DATE DUE			

WITHDRAWN

Media
and
Change

Media
and
Change

Edited by

J. A. F. van Zyl and K. G. Tomaselli

McGRAW-HILL BOOK COMPANY, JOHANNESBURG

NEW YORK   ST. LOUIS   SAN FRANCISCO   AUCKLAND   BOGOTÁ
DÜSSELDORF   LONDON   MADRID   MEXICO   MONTREAL
NEW DELHI   PANAMA   PARIS   SÃO PAULO   SINGAPORE
SYDNEY   TOKYO   TORONTO

301.161

M46

115527

Sept. 1980

Set in 10/12 Times Roman
Typesetting and design by C.T.P.
Printed and bound by Cape & Transvaal Printers Ltd., Cape Town

Table of Contents

Foreword

At any time, the evolution of any sector of any discipline is to a large extent dependent upon the interests and orientations of its students, and their respective connections and interactions with researchers in allied fields. Central themes of some considered importance when first mooted become outmoded or are superseded as the years pass. In some disciplines, change is smooth, continuous and chronological. Other fields exhibit a series of seemingly unrelated progressions and shifts which seem to be independent of unifying concepts or frameworks. Not solely part of any one academic field and not unified enough to constitute a recognized discipline within itself, such knowledge remains under-utilized, and largely non-integrated into a general body of knowledge. One such example is communications science, which, except for certain transformations based upon particular works, continues to tread a path in the academic wilderness. Specific works have led to the creation of particular paradigms which researchers have utilized in their pursuit of normal scientific activity. The two basic offerings which have to some extent fused the discipline of communications are widely differing, although complementary in the ideas presented. The writings of Marshall McLuhan and Norbert Wiener represent the two basic transformations which have led to the recognition of communications as a science. The ideas originally expounded by these two writers are developed in the chapters that follow, and it is interesting to note that although many innovative works have subsequently appeared, few if any have synthesized the whole field of communications, their subject matter being concerned rather with sub-parts of the communications system.

In more than a decade of research since the first appearance of McLuhan's book *Understanding Media* the dominant problem still confronting the communications scientist is the fragmented approach and undefined status of communications studies.

Students of communication have looked at what the field has produced in the past, and noting the non-emergence of a unified framework, its lack of integration and its apparent non-ability to explain or predict important problems, they have retreated and become academically introspective. They have shied away from an inter-disciplinary approach and have not asked relevant or new questions, this resulting in a multitude of definitions of the "discipline" communications.

Expanded Cinema written by Gene Youngblood represents one of the few recent works which attempt to place the communications process in perspective in terms of human society. Although Youngblood's style of writing has been criticized as ". . . that blathering style common among media freaks – half Bucky Fuller and half McLuhan 'probes' – with a peculiarly alarming Teutonic tendency toward agglomeration" we, along with this critic,[1] agree that his thesis is important, although possibly for different reasons. The importance of *Expanded Cinema* lies not in its unusual methodology, but rather in its continual and unrelenting questioning of existing paradigms, concepts, theories and attitudes. It is surprising therefore that we are aware of only one reference made to this book.

The present volume presents an interdisciplinary approach and questions the sometimes naïve and often bland concepts upon which much communications knowledge is grounded. Although the writers are drawn from widely differing backgrounds, the basic themes and concepts are remarkably similar, and the conclusions of one chapter are expanded upon in the body of the next. The content moves from an examination of the theoretical underpinnings in the arts to the application of related processes in scientific research, communications, city and regional planning. New communications technologies imply new messages. New messages create new forms of human interaction. Changing forms of communication generate new social processes which in turn determine the evolution of city structure.

The first chapter presents a general overview of the media and examines the argument that the illiterate of the future will not be those who cannot read, but those who cannot see. This paper explores the need for and function of a common language of vision referring specifically to film and television.

Chapter 2, building upon the conclusions in the psychological realm of the first chapter, represents a plea against the simple reading of any social situation, as if events, and social action can be divided into discontinuous and isolated digital units.

The two schools of thought concerning the effects of mass media upon modern society forms the basis of Chapter 3, while Chapter 4 deals specifically with a particular medium, still photography, and the almost dehumanizing effects that this medium has exerted on social attitudes.

Posing the question, what influence will telecommunications media as technological environments have on the spatial dimensions of cities and on the life-styles of people, Chapter 5 examines processes and questions the acceptability of the aspatial city of the 21st century.

Chapter 6 deals with the evolution of communication in individuals and societies based on the processes of neurophysiological and psychological research. The rate of an individual's or society's experiential and consciousness evolution is related to the degrees of advancement and interconnectivity of the communication networks within a specific community.

The basic conclusion of Chapter 7 is tangential to that of Chapter 1 where the author argues that our technology has outrun our mental capacity to handle its wider, human repercussions. In contrast, Chapter 8 assumes that telecommunications media will ultimately help to solve the problems of urban and rural America and presents an overview of a vast co-ordinated study of a particular area in the United States. The significance of this chapter lies in the desire to translate theory into pragmatic action.

The concluding chapter examines some aspects of the "utopia or oblivion" thesis, draws attention to other schools of thought and places the works of some media scientists and futurists in perspective.

K.G.T.

1. Callenbach, E.: "Recent Film Writing: a Survey" in *Film Quarterly*, Vol. 24, No. 3, Spring 1971 pp. 11-33

1

A general theory of intermedia communications

Keyan Tomaselli *was born in 1948 and studied at the University of the Witwatersrand, Johannesburg where he obtained a B.A. with geography and sociology majors. He graduated with B.A. (Hons) in 1974 having specialized in economic and urban geography. He is a lecturer in film production techniques in the School of Dramatic Art. During his undergraduate years he was an active film-maker on campus and was appointed the first chairman of the Wits TV Society.*

In 1974 he was appointed Film Producer for a film production house specializing in audio-visual communications and advertising. Keyan subsequently became a freelance producer and amongst other positions was appointed Supervising Producer on international partnership productions for H. d. H. Films (South Africa) (Pty.) Ltd. and company director for Indaba Sound (Pty.) Ltd., a film sound studio, and also of Indaba Films (Pty.) Ltd.

Introduction

"The amphitheatre had been designed to hold the entire waking population of Diaspar, and scarcely one of its ten million places was empty . . . it (the amphitheatre) was merely a pattern of electronic charges, slumbering in the memory of the central computer until the need came to call it forth. Alvin knows that in reality he was still in his room, and that all the myriads of people who appeared to surround him were equally in their own rooms. As long as he made no attempt to move from his spot, the illusion was perfect."[1]

The shape of things to come? Science fiction? A blurring of the distinction between illusion and reality? The two-dimensional flat earth world of the middle ages when superseded by the three dimensional revelations of Galileo evoked a myriad of horrors for the philosophers of his time. The genesis of four-dimensional man occurred with the exegesis of Darwin and was reinforced by the abstract splendour of Einstein's general

1

theory of relativity. That the "survival of the fittest" transcends the boundaries of time is encapsulated in the words of Thorday, "The fit are those who fit their existing environment and whose descendants will fit future environments."[2] Robert Ardrey has written: "We are not only what we are but what we once were."[3] He has charged certain sciences with dedicating their efforts to the proposition that man is three-dimensional, and that he owes nothing of his behaviour, thoughts and actions to anything but circumstances of his environment, as experienced during his lifetime. While Ardrey and the newly established school of sociobiologists battle against an unrelenting tide of leftist dogma, certain media prophets like Buckminster Fuller, Marshall McLuhan and Gene Youngblood propose the notion of adaptability which is independent of an ethological derivation. This volume deals with man's response to the environments he has created for himself and documents the effects that future forms of communication will exert on social processes, living and working patterns, and urban form in relation to visual literacy, differing cultural perceptions, media content and man/machine relationships. Interrelated with this theme is an investigation of Robert Ardrey's *Territorial Imperative* concepts, in contrast to Buckminster Fuller's *Utopia or Oblivion* thesis. Is man genetically pre-programmed to cause his destruction? Are his cities simply a sublimation of his killing instinct or is man adaptable and will he be able to apply his intelligence, technology and resources to create happiness and abundance for all? What are the implications for computer and telesociety and will man be able to cope with the sociological and psychological changes and economic externalities that these technologies will create? Much of our technology has been constructed in a culture-free vacuum and has already shown signs of exceeding the bounds of sociological and psychological acceptance. The chapter that follows is set within a cybernetic framework and deals with visual literacy, the relationship between art and science, types of communications technologies, and describes how communications hardware and messages filter through a society.

  While the science of cybernetics has made tremendous inroads in the methodologies of a wide spectrum of disciplines, its inherent potential to span an interdisciplinary field of investigation from the intuitive inexactitudes of art to the precise mechanics of science, has yet to be fully tapped. Few publications present a comprehensive and integrated overview of cybernetic applications; many become bogged down with detail, irrelevancies and oversimplification. The result is a reinforcement of academic partition, confusion of the student and terror conjured in the collective mind of the public as they imagine alien incursions of scientifically concocted robot creatures christened with names derived from the prefix "cyb . . ." (e.g. cyborg, cybernaut, etc.) Concepts, theories and methodologies become suspect as the jargon machine works overtime to service fleeting ideas, market demands, unresearched theses and incorrect assumptions. Confusion increases and communication decreases. The distinction between gibberish and terminology blurs and the student has to wave a white flag in an effort to save himself. How and when, where and why are certain terms used and what information does such terminology impart? When is terminology jargon or jargon terminology? The arguments in the chapters that follow have led the various authors into many diverse fields and in their writings are terms which, while they may sound jargonistic, are nevertheless scientifically tested and academically acceptable. Such words impart, concisely and efficiently, specific meanings which may otherwise consume several pages, if not chapters, in explanation. Jargon refers to unintelligible gibberish while scientific language refers to specifically defined meanings and concepts.

K.G.T.

1. Clark, A. C.: *The City and the Stars*. Corgi, London, 1957, p. 234
2. Thorday, J. M.: "Natural Selection and Biological Progress", in *A Century of Darwin* (ed. S. A. Barnett), 1958
3. Ardrey, R.: "Four-Dimensional Man." *Encounter*, Vol. 38, No. 2, Feb. 1972, pp. 9-21

A general theory of intermedia communications

Existing in many countries are preliterate societies and rural communities which are unable to comprehend three-dimensional drawings, perceive the relationships in a perspective diagram or discern the relative sizes of familiar objects in different environments. They are quite likely to evacuate a cine hall in terror to avoid the image of an oncoming train or alternatively, to peer behind the screen to establish the image's origin. These communities can be contrasted with the literate and more visually educated urban culture which has acquired an ability to read pictures, understand perspective, and, to a certain extent to discern visual reality from illusion. However, many people still have little or no conception of the role of visual understanding in our advanced technological society.

The retina is a specialized surface of the brain and an estimated 75% of information enters the brain through the eyes. Although able to comprehend on a verbal level, most individuals in modern society, due to their underdeveloped visual perception, are unable to assess and comprehend the images and environments created for them by mediators such as film-makers, television producers, painters, architects and townplanners. Faced with a multiplicity of visual information, an endless variety of forms, colours, textures, rhythms, visual and spatial relationships, the art objects of the past and the manifestations of the present, the individual is bewildered. To interpret the confusion of styles represented in present-day architecture for example, evaluation should encompass not only physical and economic attributes (the influence of property economics on architectural design) but also symbolic and aesthetic qualities. The imitations of the past built for the functions of the present, suggest an inability on the part of the mediator to extend the limits of his architectural language, because, as his creative awareness and perceptual ability are *not* developed, his tendency to imitate increases.

The urgency of studying the phenomenon of vision and visual communication is underlined by the increasing use of channels (all forms of audio-visual hardware, e.g. TV, film, teaching machines and OHPs) in the instruction of school children by teachers (or mediators) who are uneducated in the general language of vision. Against this background and that of rapid technological advance in film and television and their respective software systems and languages, it may be argued that the illiterate of the future will not be those who cannot read, but those who cannot see.

A *language of vision*

The initial movement towards a common language of vision as a unifying agent of the arts was headed by the Bauhaus school pioneered by Gropius.[1] He sought to establish the root of all the arts through a study of design activities and aesthetic fundamentals in order to define a common language of communication between artist and community. In support, Sash[2] has emphasized that such a frame of reference, incorporating a common visual-aesthetic language of colour, shapes, forms and visual relationships, will assist the individual to perceive as an artist does, without necessarily participating in the action of creating images.

The differences in the languages of the various manifestations of vision such as film and television are essentially those associated with symbol formation and arrangement. Language is a process which generates symbols and involves the use of conventions as well as the establishment and creation of forms and patterns by the mediator. Thus an appreciation of the type of images suitable to various media, and of the methods by which the mediator enlists the attributes of a medium to enhance his message, may be developed. Further, as Gropius implied by subscribing to the same theory, the various media can impart their several messages in a coherent and cogent manner; thus they become unified in the observer.

Film as Art

The attributes of film are two-fold. Film is *accessible* in the sense that even the most complex films are comprehensible on the *primary level* of recognition and understanding, e.g. in *Citizen Kane* and *O Lucky Man* cars, furniture, people and a multiplicity of other objects are recognizable. Accessibility causes passivity. The individual might not subject the film to his cognitive process, the second step of understanding communication which embraces perception, evaluation, reasoning and assessment in an effort to elicit meaning. On this *secondary level* themes, patterns and messages may pass undetected and in this respect perception of the film may be negligible. This happens because cognition is selectively organized and because the cognitive map of an individual is not a photographic representation of the physical world, but is rather a partial, personal construction in which certain objects, singled out by the individual for a major role, are perceived in an individual manner. Thus the perceiver paints a picture of the world (or experience) that expresses his individual view of reality.[3]

The process of learning to see films at this secondary level is the process of learning to go beyond accessibility. Film is able to produce subliminal effects. The viewer does not count the length of shots as the excitement mounts to see if increasingly rapid cutting is causing the effect.[4] The consequent ability of the film-maker to structure the visual content of the film so as to elicit particular psychological responses from the audience leads to the realization that the film and television media are not neutral carriers of whatever information is committed to them. Further, while the content of many films may appear to be plausible due to an initial emotive impact the intellectual response must not be overlooked, for an in-depth examination of the ideas and arguments conveyed might well demonstrate that certain concepts, assumptions and conclusions of the film or film-maker may be simplistic, naïve or even misleading when evaluated in terms of the spectator's previous knowledge and experience.

Thus an understanding of film at the secondary level enhances visual literacy and increases the probabilities of an instantaneous response being accurate. A spectator's ability to read a film (or to understand media) depends upon his ability to decode the message, the primary level being recognition and understanding. The sub-components of the code are arranged into patterns and are evaluated in terms of the spectator's own experience as he constructs for himself a meaningful world.

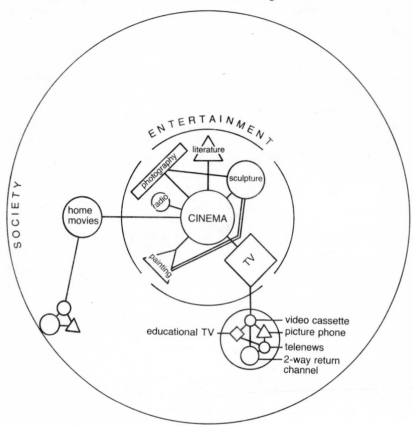

Figure 1. A communications system

The following section deals with art and entertainment as a system and its control by the application of cybernetic principles. Entertainment is defined as "agreeably occupying" the time of the spectator or as "amusement". A system is a set of interconnected parts, each part a system in itself, each system contained within a larger system, and so on (Fig. 1). Control may be defined as intervention which restricts deviations from system objectives or goals to within acceptable limits. Cybernetics is the study of the control of complex systems. This general definition can be applied to any control situation in both the human and physical sciences whether or not the system is simple and determinate or probabilistic and highly complex.

A cybernetic analysis of communication

There is a tendency for studies which embrace cybernetics to shy away from a clear definition of the processes and applications within the system under investigation, and to jump directly into a discussion of both, a procedure which may tend to confuse the student. This analysis has attempted to identify the components and interactions of a cybernetic system and will define the system in question. The control process is based on a feedback loop through which the *output* of a system is linked to its *input* in such a way that variations in output from some pre-set norm or goal results in compensatory behaviour that tends to restore the system output to that goal. Control on the basis of actual performance rather than expected performance is known as error-controlled regulation or feedback, and involves sensory mechanisms which monitor and indicate performance. The actual performance of the system is compared with the intended performance (or goal) and *information* is returned to the decision-making point so that the inputs can be modified to correct the system output to within the limits set. The sensory mechanism must have a capacity to anticipate and monitor disturbances which may arise from the system's environment. The decision-making device must specify action which will effectively deal with the disturbances to keep the system viable and enable it to produce an output which is within acceptable limits.

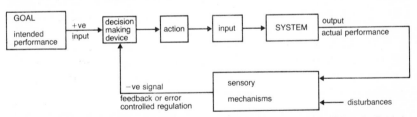

Figure 2. A cybernetic system. In any system the input signal is positive. When feedback is introduced to stabilize a system, the feedback signal contains a negative charge

The variety in the decision-making device must be at least equal to that of the disturbances. The decision-making device functions to control the natural tendency of closed systems to deteriorate and to become disordered by adjusting the system's parts to within narrow pre-established limits.

Purposeful behaviour is the final condition in which the behaving system reaches a definite correlation in time or space with respect to a relatively specific goal.[5] Cybernetic systems then, require perception of deviation from the intended performance or goal, decision making and action to correct the deviation (Fig. 2).

Entropy

The central notion which underlies the concept of entropy is the extent to which solutions offered to questions about one set of systems are probable among a larger set of systems. In physical terms, entropy defines the quantity of energy reversibly exchanged between one system in the universe and another. According to the Law of Entropy (or 2nd Law of Thermodynamics) the probability of energy exchange increases as the universe grows older. Entropy is a measure of this probability. The Second Law of Thermodynamics states that as entropy increases, the universe and the order existing within all closed systems tend naturally to deteriorate and lose their distinctiveness. They move from a state of organization and differentation to a state of chaos and sameness.[6]

This process is, however, not valid for contiguous parts of the universe in which local and temporary enclaves of decreasing entropy or increasing organization exist. This counter-process is due to an exchange of information from the smaller system to the larger system. Information is the content of what is exchanged with the larger system as the smaller system adjusts to it, and makes its adjustment felt upon it. To exist effectively is to exist with adequate information. Entropy, then, not only measures the disorder of a system but also the lack of information about the *structure of the system*. An adequately informed system generates sufficient energy to facilitate change and assert progress. Energy is defined as the "capacity to re-arrange elemental order"[7] and runs counter to entropy which has no such capacity as no information is returned through the input channels. The amount of energy generated is directly proportional to the amount of information available about the system.

Wiener in expanding the above to include human communication, writes ". . . it is possible to treat sets of messages as having an entropy – like sets of states of the external world . . . the information carried by a set of messages is a measure of organization. In fact, it is possible to interpret the information carried by a message as essentially the negative of its entropy . . ."[8] That is, the less anticipated the message, the more information it gives. Clichés, for example, are less illuminating than great poems.

The phenomenon of man and his process of interaction with other men and communications media should involve a regenerative negative entropy relationship. This negentropic condition results from the feedback process since the sub-parts of the system feed energy back into one another resulting in cumulative reactions.

Entropy and Film

Following Youngblood,[9] film, art and entertainment constitute a cybernetic system in the following terms: "structure of the system" refers to the human condition as defined by D. H. Lawrence: "The business of art is to reveal the relation between man and his circumambient universe . . ."[10] Entropy refers to the degree of man's ignorance about his condition. Ignorance is a state of increasing chaos due to misinformation or lack of information about the structure of the system. Plot, story and drama are the decision-making or control devices which enable the commercial entertainer to adjust the inputs and so manipulate the output or the audience. Chaos is a state of least order and increased sameness. The basic assumption underlying Youngblood's analysis is that the goal of cinema should not be to entertain, but to inform man of his condition. His analysis is inflexible and cannot take cognizance of contradictory behaviour within interacting systems. His use of the term entropy is somewhat loose and possibly misleading in certain instances. Nevertheless his conclusions are sound and it is the intention of the present discussion to clarify and develop his ideas.

Visual Understanding

In terms of film, the purpose of cybernetic analysis is to determine what inputs (or success formulae) are required to achieve sufficient outputs (profit) given a set of goals. Within such a framework the concepts of art and entertainment can be classified into three processes:

1. System-maintaining;
2. evolutionary; and
3. revolutionary.

1. System maintaining: This involves repetitive action which eliminates deviationist tendencies through negative feedback and serves to maintain steady state patterns. This self-adapting process provides complex closed systems that tend to suppress change. These systems (e.g. entertainment) tend for a time to maintain this stable level of organization, as a local island in a general stream of increasing entropy (society at large). One rather shallow definition of art falls within this category. ". . . art is a process in which the artist makes use of his experience, intuition or inspiration, selecting and arranging it to create beautiful and true artistic objects which

to a greater or lesser extent imitate reality and through these objects he communicates his experience to an audience."[11]

Two issues concern us here:

a. ". . . beautiful and true . . ." suggest a steady state maintenance of a passive mode of indulgence on the part of the spectator. If art communicates the human condition and this condition is not necessarily beautiful, then the negative feedback will eliminate such unwanted communication.

b. ". . . imitate reality . . ." Imitation is the result of inadequate information and is repetitive and stable within its narrow confines in that no attempt is made to reassess or expand human experience. No new information is returned via the feedback loop. No cognizance is taken of outside disturbances and no change in system behaviour results. The system is therefore unable to develop or match the variety of disturbances which may occur. The nature of disturbances which may impinge upon the system may cause it to decay at a greater rate than it can reconstitute itself, e.g. it became evident that the silent movie, as constructed by the Russian School, had evolved towards a dead end, its capacity for mutation and adaption declined through its strict adherence to overspecialized norms (or stability), and an inability to cope with a new disturbance, sound (Fig. 3).

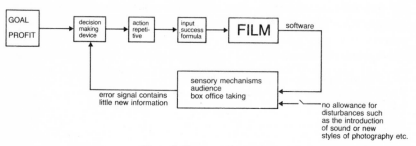

Figure 3. System maintenance

Youngblood has argued that commercial entertainment is non-creative, destroys the audience's ability to appreciate and participate in the creative process and works against art since it is a closed system where the feedback process is dominated by a lack of information. That is, the error feedback signal contains information which is highly repetitive and highly probable. In other words, to satisfy the profit motive the commercial entertainer must give the audience what it expects (he must speak a common language) which is conditional upon what this audience previously received. Youngblood compares the term "genre" to a level of probability: "The content of westerns, gangster movies, romances, etc. is probable in that it can be identified and comprehended simply by classification."[12] Opposed to change, the entertainer, who is but a craftsman, tries not to alienate his audience by employing a new language even if he were capable of it. A pertinent example is Alfred Hitchcock's[13] statement, "In recent years . . . I have become more commercially minded, afraid that anything at all subtle may be missed. I have learned from experience how easy small touches are overlooked . . . The art of directing for the commercial market is to know just how far you can go . . ." Thus Hitchcock at any point in time is only utilizing a convention of dramatic manipulation in order to supply the temporary gratification that commercial entertainment offers the audience. Such information is repetitive, non-informative and stable.

2. Evolutionary: Some systems exhibit an ability to increase their level of organization. Events in this category to a small extent transcend pre-conditioned response formulas to produce growth and progressive change by amplifying negative feedback in the system. This process has a capacity for self-transformation into new and different styles through introducing a variety which permits constructive change. Hence Hitchcock[14] can say, "I am freer now to do what I want than I was just a few years ago." This explains why films which seem incomprehensible on first release are understood better some years afterwards by the same audiences who have, in the interim, benefited from the regenerative negative and cumulative feedback. In other words the audience has increased in film literacy. The variety of disturbances in the real world are adequately matched by the variety in the decision-making device and the system has learned to predict from the feedback process. Perhaps the most stunning example of the upper limit of this form of negentropy in the film world applies to the response of critics to Orson Welles' *Citizen Kane*. Although this film was released in 1941 Gottesman[15], three decades later has commented ". . . it is only in the past decade that anything like genuine analysis and criticism has begun to acknowledge and try to come to terms with the heft, complexity, and resonance of this extraordinary act of imagination. This is not to say . . . that *Citizen Kane* is now fully – or even adequately – accounted for. The film . . . still contains many mysteries . . . we have got beyond its first 'No Trespassing' sign . . ." Although this example may be a little strong for inclusion under the title evolutionary, it does nevertheless clearly explain the concept of self-transformation. In cybernetic terms, the more information that the artist is able to transmit, the greater the degree of negentropy and the greater the ability of the artist to create, and the audience to accept change.

3. Revolutionary: This category defines the nature of art in that sequences are set in motion that transform the system by redefining its languages, limits, styles and types of interactions. Here the artist, a visionary, a catalyst of change, is always engaged in writing a detailed account of the future because he is one of the few people aware of the nature of the present. He often produces new symbols, new structures and new properties in his attempt at diagnosis, definition and rationale of the human condition. Under these circumstances negentropy is at its highest, and the potential for change at its greatest. "The notion of experimental art . . . is meaningless. All art is experimental or it isn't art. Art is research . . ."[16]

Just as sculpture is the art of space and music is the art of time so the space-time movements of film in terms of light, object and camera together yield infinite varieties of plastic form. Read has asserted that the true plasticity of film, the plasticity which gives the film its uniqueness, is a plasticity of light. An essential film would be an abstract film, a "pure" creation of light and darkness, just as an essential painting is an abstract painting. Unfortunately, Read undervalues his own thesis in his statement: "But such films are only for the purists."[17] New technological extensions have led to the birth of new cinematic forms which must include video-tronics, computers and laser light. The first generation of electrovideo-graphic artists has emerged and people such as Jordan Belson, the Whitney brothers, John Stehura, Jerry Riley and many others are redefining the limits of film far beyond the accepted traditional styles.

In order for a system to develop, the sensory mechanisms must be able to sense threatened disturbances, estimate and anticipate their effects and deal appropriately with them. Action must be specified to take advantage of perceived real world situations. The revolutionary process tends initially towards conflict because it has to break through an already established stable system, but eventually settles down at a higher level of order and purpose (Fig. 4). As the system ages, this level of order is subject to the law of diminishing returns and the negentropy decreases until eventually it subsists at the system-maintaining level or even degenerates into an entropic condition. Nevertheless, through the initial impulse the hierarchy of levels of order and purpose in the universe are constantly upgraded with respect to the isolated closed systems which characterize the notions of art and entertainment. Events set in motion by the revolutionary process, however, are highly subject to the danger of becoming entropic as the profit-orientated entertainer utilizes the structures since discarded by the artist in his search for new visions. American reaction to Antonioni's film *Blow Up* provides an example of this kind of process.

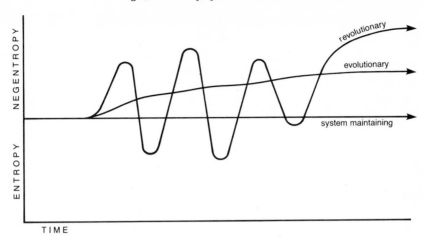

Figure 4. Entropy

Antonioni had anticipated a lessening of restrictions with regard to previously censorable material. He reacted with an unexpected boldness in the rendering of some nude sex scenes to take advantage of the expected introduction of the X-rated category in American cinemas.

Probably no other film made in the early 1960s stimulated as wide a range of responses. Reaction, ranging from banning demands, strong disapproval, being upheld as a moral lesson by a Protestant church to taking the best film of the year award, charted the film's initial contradictory interpretations.[18]

Since 1966 the release of far more sexually explicit films such as *I am Curious, Censorship in Denmark* have appeared, each in turn displaying less content but more explicit sex, each film becoming less distinctive as the curve becomes entropic, and so on down the entropy curve until it flattened out with a worse than amateur production in the form of *Deep Throat*. (Fig 5).

On the other hand, the higher level of order established by films which fall into the revolutionary category provide the foundation from which the next leap is taken. D. W. Griffith was possibly the first film artist, his film *The Birth of a Nation* being a watershed because:

1. It initiated an era of cinematic propaganda;
2. It heralded the age of film as a socio-political commentary;
3. Public reaction, violent controversy, censorship demands and riots elevated the popular image of the cinema from crude entertainment to that of a significant and powerful means of expression.

Society is subject to the Second Law of Thermodynamics: Confusion

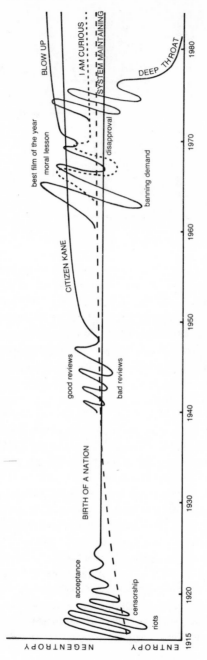

Figure 5. Entropy graph of selected films

increases and order decreases. Although the three systems described above are potentially stable or negentropic and regenerative when studied in isolation, in terms of the larger system of life, they are but enclaves in a deteriorating, entropic world. Griffith had revealed the human condition of his time and his audience responded predictably. The information content of his film was too high, people were not conditioned for what they saw and sought refuge and escape by instituting more sensitive sensory mechanisms in the form of censorship and other regulating techniques. That is, the amount of energy or information reversibly exchanged from the smaller to the larger system was reduced to acceptable societal limits, and the potential for change in the larger system diminished.

There are, however, other processes operating which, interlinking with the progressing language of vision, have led to different media obtaining full art status. The pace of change in our society is such that ". . . different generations living side by side may now . . . live in essentially different (but overlapping) cultural epochs".[19] Cinema and television are essentially two historically distinct media which function side by side serving overlapping audiences.

The consequences are that every medium tends to become the content of the medium which succeeds it historically. Thus books (particularly novels) become the content of films and films become the content of television. Photography has freed Western painting from its obsession with realism and has allowed it to gain its autonomy. Similarly television is the major cause for the emergence of the art movie, since the small electronic screen has usurped many of the journalistic functions previously performed by film. Each of the above media is a system in itself, while interacting and contained within a larger system. Certain of the parts or enclaves may exhibit a direction opposed to that of the universe at large. Progress finds its home in some of these enclaves. Painting, sculpture, films, TV, photography, etc. may be regarded as islands of evolutionary or revolutionary organization contained within the larger system of steady state entertainment, itself nesting within the system of human society. (Fig. 1).

Traditionally, the artist's artefacts mirror his discoveries of his environment and reflect his search for order from chaos. Systems of classification, artistic modes, myths and legends all represent attempts to gain an insight into the conditions governing the artist's order. The source of this order is dual: it is understood either as an inherent part of nature, requiring discovery by man, or it is argued that order comes from within man, that is, he imposes order on the world around him. No man-made system can avoid the arbitrary; no system of analysis will ever be conclusive because man does not know the ultimate cause of events. The artist ranks his facts and integrates his vision according to the structures important to him. Fundamental in the search for relationship and order is the acknowledgement "It is not true that man must supply the world with an organizing principle! It already exists . . . Nature works according to laws, but man acts according to his idea of laws."[20] In other words, whether or not order exists in the external world, man's perception of that order is of his own creating. The questions to be posed are: How are relationships established between the language of vision and the external world? What is the relationship between the artist's understanding of the nature of the present and the mathematical order external to man?

Visual Education and Science

Art is a vehicle for communication and enables a society to create and transmit a distinctive culture through a unity of visual perception. Read asserts that during the great periods of civilization a fundamental unity of vision controlled all that was made and done – even down to rituals, parades and pageants. The artist, impelled by his creative spirit toward synthesis, needs to achieve a creative unity of a higher order of structure, value and purpose.[21] Read, Gropius and Sash contend that this unifying power is lost in our world of ever-increasing specialization. The recent innovation of Art History as an academic discipline, previously a neglected area of study, coupled with the observation that in education the new audio-visual systems are being used as twentieth century channels to convey a conceptual context which is still nineteenth century or earlier[22] and the non-development of an overriding style of art that springs spontaneously from the basic social and economic realities of our way of life suggests a disintegration of this visual unity. In the search for new visions, artists now create visual images without "object" matter which the visually uneducated spectator is unable to read. The language of science represents an extreme degree of specialization in the direction of a mathematical precision.

Such precision is possible only in relation to certain materials and can be gained only by using terms in special and previously defined senses.[23] Art also represents a specialization of language for the purpose of precision but does not exclude as science does communication via associations, emotional colourings and implications of attitude and judgement. Language is the foundation for man's ability to solve problems and is also the springboard for misunderstandings because of the lack of adequate structures to interpret both the artistic and scientific languages simultaneously. As Alice said, "How can I know what I think till I see what I say."

The polarity between art and science is a genetic factor, for their respective derivations, although probably sharing a common historical ancestry, went on to develop along divergent paths. Cohen states that the artist's (mental) model is given and he accepts it as he finds it. His task is to match reality to this model in whatever medium he works.[24] Conversely, the scientist constructs a model to match nature and modifies it when necessary. For him nature is given. However, despite these opposing standpoints the *rapprochement* of art and science is normatively feasible since if scientific technology is able to alter the realm of what can be done, and art reveals nature as it is, the domain of what ought to be done can be defined. The influence of technological innovations of the media, such as the various forms of film and television, can effect decisions on desirable ends as well as suggesting new means of attaining those ends. In other words, the duty of a language of vision is not only to explain reality, but also to improve it. Our understanding of urban phenomena could, for example, be extended by the use of computer films, which, using conventional mathematical models and various gaming techniques as inputs, can simulate alternative visual futures. In one such film, *City-Scape*, mathematical equations describe a three-dimensional environment which is transformed onto a two-dimensional colour television display screen. The properties of the visual display include true perspective, controlled colour and brightness and infinite depth of focus. The spectator, by manipulating a control of the computer is able to drive a vehicle through the city to the extent that while moving north he is able to turn around and view what has been behind him in the south. In this way a strong sense of location and environment are created for the driver/ spectator.[25] Youngblood[26] has commented that such films "create facts, not myths which obscure the boundaries between life and art with a scientific finality unequalled in subjective art".

An evolving discipline of mathematical aesthetics (in the Kantian sense) would assist in the evaluation of the city produced in *City-Scape*. The aesthetic elements would be pre-established and their appearance, distribution and form described in mathematical terms. The elements should incorporate sensuous qualities such as sounds, colours, tones, textures as well as meanings deduced from objects, form and design. A pyramid of degrees of quality could be constructed incorporating economic, visual value, symbolic and aesthetic variables.

The creator of *City-Scape* is attempting to translate the results generated by one language (computer language) into another language (visual language). These translations facilitate interpretation of the implications of one style of analysis for another style of analysis. Although both languages represent different ways of saying the same thing, when structures are established to handle both languages simultaneously (as in *City-Scape*) the communicative qualities of the new medium assist in a greater understanding. The result is an extension of our language and a new analytical category to facilitate a greater understanding of reality.

The application of even more probabilistic computer film techniques than those applied in the making of *City-Scape* can provide the means by which new objectives can be formulated, e.g. to evaluate the future shape of cities, a simulation over time of the effects and feedback of various inputs (e.g. changing economic, sociological and communicative technologies, aesthetic and other dynamic variables) will produce a dynamic visual colour television display. Such visual data can optimize community involvement in the planning process, for pictures are quicker and easier to evaluate than the abstract data spewed out on miles of computer printout.

In the words of *City-Scape's* creator, Peter Kamnitzer,[27] ". . . we would like to put the researcher, designer, decisionmaker or the public in an environment where they could be exposed to what various futures may look like".

A consequence is the evolution of the science of art which aims at identifying order and logic in a confused universe. Although the artist may be intuitively able to make his ideas clear, they may lack objective validity because he has not applied scientific logic. The next area of study is how to co-ordinate the creative ideas of the artist with the technologically conversant scientist. A mathematical-artistical connection requires an idea, and a common language to express the ideas through logic, reasoning, analysis and the formulation of goals and objectives, as well as a set of visual structures for recording the result. In conjunction with this evolving science an understanding of the language of vision, a theoretical grounding in art, and a technological ability to manipulate media and machines may in part presage the technological artist who in contradistinction to the pure artist does not rely on the intuitive, emotive and random procedures which have typified the creative process to date. If the content of media is art, and art is the creation of a new world, never seen before, imperceptibly gaining on reality[28] then the solutions offered by artists (including the technological artist) create some of the problems of the future.

On a more practical level, how can art (films, television, computer movies, etc.) assist in the solution and prediction of problems? Consider the geography of time and space. Geography students are taught the principles of spatial location by means of maps, geometry, and spatial organization theories with respect to city, region and country. The study of spatial organization is past and present orientated and lacks an aesthetic dimension. The students learn the locations of capital cities, rivers, of agrarian and industrial revolutions, of rainfall, vegetation and cultural regions and respective dates where applicable. They do not learn the aesthetic principles of spatial organization which have been postulated by Langer[29] who has distinguished between the space in which we live and the space of art. The former is not art at all but rather a system of economic, geographical, sociological and political relationships, whereas the latter is a created space built out of forms, colours and shapes. Nevertheless the shaping of space in reality is symbolic of our culture, of the existing social order and of society's aspirations. To evaluate spatial form in art or reality requires an understanding of the symbolic qualities intrinsic in that form.

If we are to solve the problems of tomorrow, and to understand how the artistic perceptions of tomorrow become the problems of the post-tomorrow, images of the future cannot be based on the illogic and chaos and the ''pretence towards scientific accuracy''[30] evident in past-orientated science fiction conventions of comic strips and films such as *Flash Gordon* and *Superman*. The student must discern accurate images of future trends and directions. Film as art can, however, assist through its creative atrributes to stimulate curiosity and so move education into a futuristic framework. One such film, an essentially non-verbal experience, is *2001: A Space Odyssey*, written by Arthur C. Clarke, a space scientist. He is concerned with man's hierarchical position in the universe and his reaction to the discovery of a higher intelligence. The spectator is led through a futurist but plausible exploration of the mire of political, psychological, ethical and geographical issues that may face future generations. Man's solution to the identification of the monolith (an artifact connected with an extra-terrestrial intelligence) was HAL, a computer. The solution becomes a problem when HAL malfunctions, and the solution to this problem is effected when the spaceman becomes a ''star child'' on another level of existence. Even this becomes a problem. ''For though he was the master of the world, he was not quite sure what to do next.''[31]

The following stage of the analysis involves a wider frame of reference and includes all types of telecommunications since communication is the basic device which makes social existence possible.

Towards a theory of intermedia communications – a general overview

Information does not appear universally at any time but manifests itself at points of information transfer, and diffuses through space in definite channels. On a global scale the intermedia network of telephone, radio, teleprinter, film, cinema, television, etc., is encapsulated in what has been termed the "noosystem" – the special environment of man consisting of the systems of organized thought and its products in which men move and have their being.[32]

Applied to our present physical level of communication this term embraces a system promoted and sustained by three and a half billion people and is serviced by more than 358 million telephone stations, 125 earth satellite tracking stations and about a billion radio and television receivers. The earth is surrounded by an invisible net of information which assumes a variety of forms including speech, still and moving images, and the language of computer data.[33] Distributed by the intermedia network, each form of communication defines its own activity space to ensure successful functioning. The lecture medium necessitates lecture theatres and school rooms, the 35 mm film medium ensures cinemas, CCTV demands a library of pre-recorded programmes and viewing spaces. Broadcast television, radio, telephone, film and video cassette systems can be found in varied environments including showrooms, sitting rooms and, increasingly, motor cars.

The advent of other media such as the picture phone, facsimile, telemail, electronic libraries, video newspapers, data access, teleconferencing, confravision, portable computer terminals in briefcase form and holography will move mankind into an era of telemobility. Already international telephony is doubling every three years, while other telecommunications services such as telex and digital transmission are exhibiting even higher growth rates.

Berry[34] has concluded that the process of telemobility will facilitate a compression of time and space with an attendant intensification of human experience alongside lessening demands for movement because of centralized information sources and instantaneous communication. In this context Servan-Schreiber has monitored the lessening time-lag between invention and manufacture. For example, the time lag was 112 years for photography (1727-1839) 56 years for the telephone (1820-76), 35 years for radio (1867-1902), 15 years for radar (1925-40), 12 years for television (1922-34), 5 years for the transistor (1948-53) and 3 years for the integrated circuit (1958-61).[35] Further developments in optical communications, wideband technologies and materials, components and equipment will serve to accelerate the pace of invention, exploitation, and diffusion through the population. This in turn lessens threshold limitations of a population, be they economic, political or behavioural, which consequently increases exposure to new media and leads to a higher rate of adoption by the individual, and the whole cycle is further accelerated.

The consequent electronically induced knowledge implosion necessitates an instantaneous internalization of knowledge and calls upon the individual to continually reassess his mental models of reality. Events are not presented in a linear sequence but are relayed in their complex immediacy through the noosystem which now facilitates a non-physical dimension of movement, e.g. telemobility, which eliminates travel and enables immediate interpersonal contact without actual presence.

An observation of such processes has led Teilhard de Chardin to comment that the whole human race is evolving towards a unity on a planetary scale, the like of which has never been known before. Such events are said to make possible the evolution of a McLuhanesque global village where the media can enlarge man's physical world and function to telescope the individual through time and space. This village will be characterized by the experience of events which are people-orientated in contrast to experience which is place-orientated. The implication in physical space terms is that the traditional distance decay concepts will be superseded by electronic technologies which will reduce the frictions of space and time delays in the diffusion of information through the intermedia network. Thus it is that the public suddenly discovers poverty in the Other America or pollution in the 1970s when in fact it was probably worse in the 1870s. Eventually, continuing sophistication in communications media will facilitate the reception of all information at an individual level.

While much of the above exposition comprises speculative elements that may exceed the evidence of available data, the function of any theory of communications is to summarize existing knowledge in terms of intermedia communications, to provide an explanation of observed events and relationships, and to predict the occurrence of as yet unobserved events and relationships on the basis of the explanatory principles embodied in the theory. Once the processes and consequences have been determined the problem is then to investigate alternative futures if the predictions portray an unacceptable future.

A discursive analysis of the way in which the diffusion of information in physical space gives way to a telemobility in non-physical space must provide the initial framework. A spatial-temporal measurement of the diffusion of information through various channels, within the framework of innovation diffusion theory, provides the basis for research. Only when the media have been distributed to a population in space, can the effects of media content be assessed.

A Redefinition of the Role of Media Sociology

The thoughts presented earlier in this chapter are infused with the notion that the integrity of the channels of visual communication is indispensible to the evolutionary growth and welfare of society. With the advent of an increasing number of new communications technologies, and their attendant problems, an urgent need has arisen for some body of systematic knowledge to assist in the assessment of the desirability of alternative societies. The discipline of sociology perhaps falls closest to this need. Unfortunately, media researchers appear to have evaded this challenge. In this connection Tudor[36] has commented that they have adopted the "mass culture thesis" as a substitute for the lack of a sociological perspective. This thesis was in essence a poor attempt at a macro-sociology of the media. Media studies have consequently failed to explore the multiple relations between the media and society.

The writings of Marshall McLuhan and more recently Gene Young-blood represent the only attempts to escape this framework. Their philosophical thoughts deal almost exclusively with the questions: What are communications and how do they affect mankind? Although McLuhan's work has been criticized as ". . . hardly a rigorous sociology . . ."[37] his thesis has yet to be proved or disproved. A refocus of research is therefore necessary if the propositions expounded by these two authors are to be scientifically tested.

The Innovation Diffusion Process: A Conceptual Framework

Structure

The four components comprising the innovation diffusion process are the innovation (media channels such as radio and television), a population, the communication process (the transfer of information), and the adoption process.

Innovations can be classified as either material (hardware) or non-material (information or software). The population consists of two classes: adopters and non-adopters. The adoption process implies growth and involves the ". . . acceptance over time of some specific idea or practice by individuals, groups or other adopting units linked to specific channels of communication, to a social structure, and to a given system of values or culture".[38] People are non-adopters either because they are unaware of the innovation or they are aware and are in the process of making a decision or they are aware and have made the decision to reject. The communication process is the means by which the innovation or information relating to the innovation is diffused through the population or society, a process which operates when a change agent or adopter communicates with an – as yet – non-adopter. In technologically advanced societies, the transmission of information occurs as follows: [39]

1. Communication is initiated by an adoption agency (e.g. television manufacturers) to induce awareness of the innovation. Historically, this function has been performed, for example, by the pony express, newspapers, telegraph, telephone, radio and more recently, television.

2. The information is received and accepted by opinion leaders who in turn influence their followers into acceptance.

In the transmission of messages from one system to another the amount of energy or information transferred decreases unless new information is fed in. The above two communication processes function primarily as persuasion and information factors. Further communication to ensure the adoption of the innovation must service both the opinion leaders and the larger part of the population who depend upon reinforcement of agency information by local important, more personal information. Termed market factors, this type of communication includes:

a. The location of distribution agencies themselves (e.g. television shops) and;
b. The shopping trip behaviour of individuals who are potential adopters (does the individual buy the innovation?)

The diffusion agency or advertiser, the individual adopter or consumer, the marketing surface, the anticipated consumer resistance, and diffusion are all interacting levels of the communications system.

Diffusion processes over time

The receipt of information transmitted via the communication process is the stimulus which elicits a response from the individual to adopt or reject an innovation. When the number of adopters is plotted against time the resultant empirical regularity is a rising S-shaped curve (Fig. 6). This graph, utilizing a logistic function, implies a contagion-type diffusion within a finite population and an adoption rate which is directly proportional to the percentages of the adopters and non-adopters: A graphical interpretation implies the existence of phases of diffusion over time, i.e. early adopters are associated with the origin phase of the S-curve, early majority and late majority adopters with the diffusion phase and laggards with the saturation phase. [40]

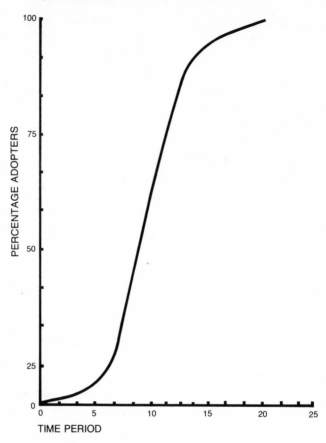

Figure 6. Diffusion of innovations through time

Diffusion in a system of cities

To understand the process of innovation diffusion theory it is necessary to be aware of the nature of the growth processes operating in any technologically advanced society. Following Berry [41] these are:

1. A system of cities, arranged in a hierarchy according to the functions performed by each;
2. Corresponding areas of urban influence surrounding each of the cities in the system.

This system of spatial organization exhibits the following characteristics:

a. The size and functions of a central city, the size of its urban field, and the spatial extent of developmental "spread effects" radiating outward from it are proportional.

b. Impulses of economic change are transmitted in order from higher to lower centres in the urban hierarchy, in a "size-ratchet" sequence, so that continued innovation in large cities remains critical for extension of growth over the complete economic system.

c. The spatial incidence of economic growth is a function of distance from the central city. Troughs of economic backwardness lie in the most inaccessible areas along the peripheries between the least accessible lower-level centres in the hierarchy.

d. The growth potential of an area situated along an axis between two cities is a function of the intensity of interaction between them.

The logical consequence of the above processes is the lessening of differences over a period of time between the cities and their peripheries, growth impulses and economic development spreading to even the most tradition-bound peripheries. For certain types of innovation (e.g. the spread of TV receivers) the more important places tend to adopt earlier than less important places, despite their relative locations, creating the hierarchy or short circuit effect.[42] This occurs because urban places are peaks on the marketing surface due to their high potential adopter density (consumer population), location of adoption agencies (television shops) and a greater probability of the existence of a TV broadcasting station.

These theses are verified by the evidence of spatial diffusion of television stations and progressively greater market penetration by the television industry in the United States between 1940 and 1968. Berry[43] identified the empirical S-shaped logistic time sequence for the installation of television stations in United States cities (Fig. 7). The diffusion pattern of stations among cities was essentially hierarchical. Larger cities or more important places installed stations before smaller cities. The proportion of households purchasing television receivers depended on the hierarchical diffusion of TV broadcasting stations, but the spatial incidence of TV receiver purchases was a function of distance from broadcasting cities, and also followed the S-shaped time sequence. Using regression analysis, Berry was able to trace the date of adoption of television stations by cities of different sizes and demonstrated that household adoption of television receivers followed a wavelike process through the urban hierarchy until some saturation level was reached. Total geographical coverage was attained by 1958 and low degrees of market penetration thereafter remained only in the nation's economically backward areas.

On this basis it may be possible to predict the diffusion times and adoption rates of future media channels and new electronic communication technologies.

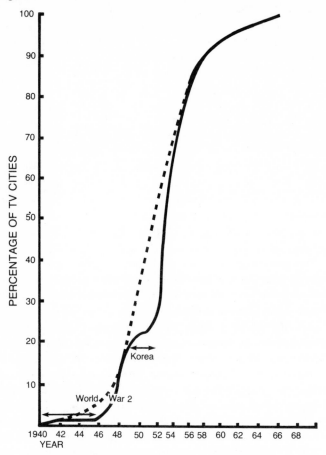

Figure 7. Growth in number of TV cities 1940–68

Function

Most important, Berry's model helps to explain the present trend from mechanical environments (dominated by spatial mobility) to electronic environments (which facilitate telemobility). The flow of innovations following the above spatial patterns, in conjunction with lessening time lags between invention (e.g. TV 1922) and manufacture (in 1934), cumulatively greater access to information resulting from the adoption of a greater variety and more efficient media channels, and a continually upgraded succession of communication systems associated with different stages of economic development and the diffusion process, together with rising real incomes will:

1. cause a lowering of threshold limitations (be they economic, social or behavioural) which will induce innovations to penetrate further down the urban hierarchy and out into the intermetropolitan periphery;

2. hasten diffusion times which will allow early adoption, which will in turn presage an increase in accessibility to information transmitted by the innovation which will tend to pre-empt the notion of distance decay to that of distance accretion. For example, persons of greater wealth may tend to work in more acceptable environments away from the social and environmental decay associated with central cities, or as Peter Goldmark envisages "Tomorrow we will communicate to our jobs".[44]

The Myth of the Global Village

The above discussion exemplifies a partial analysis of some physical processes which are operating to make the concept of the global village an empirical possibility.

Originally formalized by McLuhan[45] the concept holds that, as electrically* contracted, the globe is no more than a village bringing together all social and political functions in a sudden implosion which has heightened human awareness of responsibility intensely. Thus new communications technologies function to maintain a social system as well as make possible the symbolic sharing of human experiences, providing common understanding and a common basis for collective action.

The emergence of mass societies in the modern world occurred *pari passu* with the development of communication technologies capable of transmitting information instantaneously over large distances, supplementing communication of a direct and interpersonal nature.[46] The term "mass society", however, does not explain the rapid change initiated by the new communication instruments. Although many factors which previously worked against the emergence of a global village have been abrogated, communications mechanisms are still subject to the inexorable tendency for entropy to increase, for information to leak or distort in transit, unless certain external devices are programmed to control and monitor its transfer. Even then, unless the receiver or population exhibits an interpreting structure or organization capable of decoding incoming information, a loss of meaning or rejection may work against any action on the part of the receiving

*McLuhan should rather have used the term "electronically".

population. On a sociological level alone, the global village may be a myth, for as Timasheff has stated, "Every culture may be defined as an accumulation of inventions – technological, ideological and social. In each society, this accumulation is selective and therefore unique, never exactly repeating the accumulations made in other societies. This is why every culture has its own style . . ." [47]

A number of other complementary concepts, terms and theories have been coined to augment McLuhan's rather loose concept of the global village. Bell [48] has proposed the term, "post-industrial society" to signify the emergence of quaternary growth in a system containing five dimensions:

1. An economy based on service rather than goods-production;
2. The pre-eminence of the technical and professional classes;
3. The centrality of theoretical knowledge as the source of innovation and of policy formulation for the society;
4. The control of self-sustaining technological growth and transformation;
5. The creation of a new intellectual technology based on information and information-processing.

The above dimensions are not fully comprehensive in that they take no cognizance of the spatial component of society nor do they explain the communication processes by which the post-industrial state develops. Bell deals adequately, however, with effects. For example, he credits the change of the United States from a political entity comprising diverse areas connected by a common symbolism to a true national society, to the rise of the national network of television, coast-to-coast telephone dialling, jet transport and the simultaneous publication of national news media. Consequently the national community is subject to many common experiences ranging from the same televised sports programmes to the use of the same retail chains. The rootlessness of many Americans has elevated their experience of the national community to a higher level of importance and concern than have many of the experiences occurring at local community level. This coalescence has culminated in national efforts rather than regional or local attempts to solve social and economic problems.

Although Bell's concept offers a comprehensive statistical and analytical picture of the new information-oriented society, his inadequate treatment of the communications process must be supplemented by further research. Brzezinski's [49] "technotronic society", ". . . a society that is shaped culturally, psychologically, socially, and economically by the impact of technology and electronics – particularly in the area of computers and communications", falls short of an adequate interpretation of the social structure of society. Youngblood's "technoanarchy" in which there is no difference between the individual and the natural order (the mathematical reality external to man) is far too surrealistic for operational measurement at this stage. His assertion, "There's no semantic problem in a photographic image. We can now see through each other's eyes . . ."[50] contradicts his own argument which presupposes that communicators will perceive the same meaning in the same situations and events irrespective of their individual perceptual and cognitive differences. Youngblood's conclusion is obviously at variance with the Second Law of Thermodynamics since, according to Wiener: ". . . any transmission of, or tampering with, messages decreases the amount of information they contain, unless new information is fed in, either from new sensations or from memories which have been previously excluded from the information system".[51] Further, the individual's cognitive filter is assumed, for the purposes of Youngblood's assertions, to apply equally to all concerned in the communication process.

What has emerged however is a *planetary organization* which is united by the noosphere and its subcomponents in shared knowledge and information transfer. This organizational network, reinforced by the communications media, allows small communities with distinctive, unique or common characteristics to nest within the larger planetary social order. The larger social order still lacks the organization, sanctions and a pre-requisite network of political, economic and social systems by which a global village may be governed. Nevertheless, the noosphere does ensure that changes taking place in one section of the larger social system have immediate and repercussive effects on all other sections.

From the above investigation must evolve a new set of paradigms which will facilitate scientific investigation into the phenomenon of telemobility and its effect on mankind. The goal should be a framework in which alternative futures can be simulated so that mankind can choose the future it desires.

Alternative Futures

A number of guidelines have already emerged, these include:
1. The future communications systems should preserve the privacy of the individual.
2. Distributive communications media should incorporate return channels for individual response. The structure and function of such feedback systems have significant implications for social science and public participation in the planning process.
3. Some form of global planning must preempt the present *ad hoc* situation

to achieve an optimum economic provision of facilities to service the world's traffic streams. [52]

Further aims should encompass the following:

1. New communications technologies can close the gap between what is and what ought to be. If theory predicts that a consequence of new communication technologies will be isolation from the physical environment, from face to face relationships, and increasing isolation of the individual from social interaction, then this truth arrived at by scientific means can assist in identifying the problem. The objective is to create what is acceptable to potential system's users. If social and environmental isolation is not acceptable then the only valid policy is to eliminate the conditions which give rise to the truth of the theory.

2. Two primary models can be outlined in an approach to the study of telecommunication. [53]

    a. *The substitution model*. This is a replacement communications medium. Interaction which previously occurred through one medium (e.g. face to face meeting) is superseded by a telecommunications medium (e.g. a confravision system).

    b. The *generation model* which allows existing communication systems to remain unchanged while new communication is generated through a new medium.

    These two models are not necessarily exclusive and Tomey[54] has concluded that the use of telecommunications can in some cases lead to a *greater incidence* of face-to-face meetings, an observation contrary to much previous scholarly discussion.

3. Some principles must be formulated governing allocation of the radio frequency spectrum. TV channels make relatively heavy use of spectrum bandwidth, and capacity must be devoted to those services for which atmospheric bandwidths are the only available medium of transmission (mobile telecommunications services to aircraft, ships, cars, remote paging service, TV from satellite, space communication, etc.)

On an individual level, the tasks are less technical, more psychological. Youngblood[55] has stated that the world is not a stage, but a TV documentary, and through the medium of television, mankind is in direct contact with the human condition, and therefore the need to represent it through art falls away.

This statement is underlined, however, by those three basic assumptions which follow, none of which can be said to be universal.

1. That the mass communicator is able to interpret reality with the same understanding and perception of the great artists of our time and that he is

able to present an objective interpretation immediately;

2. That all television viewers are able to comprehend and read images portrayed on the screen as if their minds are an extension of a planetary media network, and that they are not subject to selective cognition; and

3. That artistic integrity in our present Paleocybernetic age is derived from technology. Since Youngblood's analysis is independent of an historical perspective he has misunderstood the fundamental symbolic relationship between man and machine. Certainly technology can give birth to new art forms, but sight should not be lost of the fact that the artist only *uses* technology; he is not the result of technology.

Youngblood's statement monitors an admirable situation exemplified by a rate of increasing negentropy not only of the sub-systems or enclaves but also of the larger system of human society.

Wiener,[56] however, has chosen to invest his observation within the accepted bounds of the Second Law of Thermodynamics. He states, "` . . . we are in an age where the enormous *per capita* bulk of communication is met by an ever thinning stream of total bulk of communication. More and more we must accept a standardized ineffective and insignificant product which, like the white bread of the bakeries, is made rather for its keeping and selling properties than for its food value''. As Youngblood himself has pointed out, the prevailing messages of the so-called popular media have lost their relevance because a socio-economic system that substitutes the profit motive for utility value separates man from himself and art from life. While information imparted by television may still be geared to the homogenizing of taste, other media have passed beyond the technological threshold at which stage standardization is necessary.

Youngblood's thesis also avoids the following questions:

1. That events will be selected for news-reporting in terms of their fit with pre-existing images – the more unclear the news item, the more likely it is to be reported within a general framework already established.[57]

2. That the media thrive on up-to-the-minute news releases. This function constrains the mass communicator to a superficial reporting of the latest trends, ideas and insights, often without understanding the underlying principles.

3. That the media are committed to reporting not what happens but what they think has happened or what they think should happen.

4. That news reporting is person centered and that negative events are preferred to positive events.[58]

5. That the mass communicator occupies a sensitive central position in a social network. He rejects and selects information in response to a variety

of pressures. Interpretation of information is also subject to the use of news angles, sensationalism, conflict, trivialization and lack of depth.[59] These points in turn structure possible responses and modes of action from the participators or spectators, as man encapsulates himself in the many contradictory enclaves of organized and disorganized information systems. It is this process which has caused our loss of visual unity and which has led to increasing bewilderment on the part of the individual in modern society.

Conclusion

The continual improvement of communications technologies in conjunction with the apparent lack of visual discrimination and low levels of visual literacy leads to the conclusion that the potentialities of the media to assist in greater awareness and creative growth in the case of meaningful social communication are rarely in evidence. Despite increasing and better methods of communication the system-maintaining propensity of the dominant media of film and television has enslaved mankind to a temporary gratification by commercial entertainment and has led to an inability of man to express his inarticulate sub-conscious by the extension of his visual language.

Although both art and science function to store, expand and order a greater comprehension of human experience, the media and audience have become alienated from the world of art on the one hand, and are still trying to discover the "organizing principle" on the scientific side. This has occurred because the media and audience have tended to concentrate on details and description rather than on significance. Such communication does not evoke a discriminating response from the spectator nor does it generate understanding of the message in relation to the external mathematical order, and also neglects the more important symbolical representative aspects.

On the positive side, Youngblood's statement does embody the thought that for man to experience a greater awareness in both *art and science,* he must be able to see. He must be able to see *what* conclusions are forced upon the individual and society, *how* these conclusions are disseminated, and above all, he must be able to see if he is to participate and communicate in the social, political and economic evolution of the planet earth.

FOOTNOTES

1. Gropius, W.: *The New Architecture and the Bauhaus.* Translated by P. Morton Shand, Faber & Faber, London, 1935
2. Sash, C.: "Visual Education and the Community." Arts Colloquium *The Humanities and Modern Society.* Faculty of Arts, University of the Witwatersrand, 1970
3. Krech, D., R. S. Crutchfield, and L. Ballachey: *Individual in Society.* McGraw-Hill, New York, 1962, p. 20
4. van Zyl, J. A. F.: *A Film Handbook.* Unpublished, 1972
5. Wiener, N., A. Rosenblueth and J. Bigelow: "Behavior, Purpose and Teleology." *Philosophy of Science,* 10, 1943, pp. 18-22
6. Gibbs, quoted in Wiener, N.: *The Human Use of Human Beings.* Eyre & Spottiswoode, London, 1954, p. 12
7. Youngblood, G.: *Expanded Cinema.* Studio Vista, London, 1970, p. 63
8. Wiener, *op. cit.* p. 21
9. Youngblood, *op. cit.* pp. 59-65
10. Lawrence, D. H., quoted in G. Youngblood, *op. cit.* p. 59
11. Stephenson, R. and J. R. Debrix: *The Cinema as Art.* Penguin, London, 1970, p. 17
12. Youngblood, *op. cit.* p. 64
13. Hitchcock, A.: "Direction" in R. D. McCann: *Film—a Montage of Theories.* E. P. Dutton, New York, 1966, p. 61
14. ibid. p. 61
15. Gottesman, R.: *Focus on Citizen Kane.* Prentice-Hall, Englewood Cliffs, 1971, p. 1
16. Youngblood, *op. cit.* p. 65
17. Read, H.: in R. D. McCann *op. cit.* pp. 165-170.
18. Huss, R.: *Focus on Blow Up.* Prentice-Hall, Englewood Cliffs, 1971
19. Gerbner, G.: "Mass Media and Human Communication Theory" in D. McQuail (ed.) *Sociology of Mass Communications,* Penguin, Harmondsworth, 1972
20. Lösch, A.: *The Economics of Location.* Yale University Press, New Haven, 1954, p. 94
21. Read, H.: Quoted in Sash, C., *op. cit.* p. 15
22. McHale, J.: "Information Explosion—Knowledge Implosion" in E. Schlossberg and L. Susskind (eds.): *Good News.* Columbia University Press, New York, 1968
23. Brooks, C. and R. P. Warren: *Understanding Poetry.* Holt, Rinehart and Winston, New York, 1960, p. 4
24. Cohen J.: "Creativity, Art and Ideas" in J. Reichardt (ed.): *Cybernetics, Art and Ideas.* Studio Vista, London, 1971, pp. 25-38
25. A more detailed description of *City-Scape* can be found in Youngblood, *op. cit.* pp. 250-256 and *Architectural Design,* Vol. 29, No. 9, pp. 507-508
26. Youngblood, *op. cit.* p. 252
27. Quoted in Youngblood, *op. cit.* p. 250
28. Lebel, Jean-Jacques: "On the Necessity of Violation" in *Drama Review,* Fall, 1968
29. Langer, S: *Feeling and Form: A Theory of Art.* New York, Scribner, 1953
30. Baxter, J.: *Science Fiction in the Cinema.* Paperback Library, New York, 1970
31. Clarke, A. C.: *2001: A Space Odyssey.* Hutchinson, London, 1968, p. 256
32. Huxley, J.: Introduction to P. T. de Chardin: *The Phenomenon of Man.* Fontana, London, 1967, p. 14
33. Sheno, N. V.: "Telecommunications and Development." *Proceedings,* Asia Electronic Conference, 1973 and Siemens International Telephone Statistics, 1976
34. Berry, B. J. L.: "The United States in the Year 2000." *Institute of British Geographers,* No. 51, 1970
35. Servan-Schreiber, J. J.: *The American Challenge.* Penguin, Harmondsworth, 1969

36. Tudor, A.: *Image and Influence*. George Allen & Unwin, London, 1973, pp. 137-138
37. Tudor, A.: *ibid*. p.141
38. Katz, E., M. L. Levin and H. Hamilton: "Traditions of Research in the Diffusion of Innovations." *American Sociological Review,* 28, 1963, pp. 237-252
39. Brown, L. A. and K. R. Cox: "Empirical Regularities in the Diffusion of Innovation." *Annals of the Association of American Geographers,* 61, 1971, pp. 551-559
40. ibid. pp. 551-552
41. Berry, *op. cit.* p. 43
42. Hagerstrand, T.: "The Propagation of Innovation Waves." *Lund Studies in Geography* No. B-4, 1952, p. 8
43. Berry, B. J. L.: "Hierarchical Diffusion: the Basis of Developmental Filtering and Spread in a System of Growth Centres" in N. Hansen (ed): *Growth Centres in Regional Development,* The Free Press, New York, 1972
44. Goldmark, T. C.: in Schwarz, B. N., *Human Connection and the New Media*. Prentice-Hall, Englewood Cliffs, 1973, p. 172
45. McLuhan, M.: *Understanding Media*. McGraw-Hill, New York, 1966, pp.12-13
46. Gist, N. P. and S. F. Fava: *Urban Society*. Thomas J. Crowell, New York, 1967, p. 508
47. Timasheff, N. S.: *Sociological Theory*. Random House, New York, 1967, p. 317
48. Bell, D. *The Coming of the Post Industrial State*. Heinemann, London, 1974, p. 14
49. Brzezinski, Z.: *Between Two Ages: America's Role in the Technotronic Era*. Viking, New York, 1970
50. Youngblood, *op. cit.* p. 130
51. Wiener, N.: *The Human Use of Human Beings*. Eyre & Spottiswoode, London, 1954, p. 94
52. Symposium "Whither Communications" *Australia Tele-communications Research*. (Special Issue) Vol. 7, No. 3, 1973
53. Tomey, J. F.: "The Field Trial of Audio Conferencing with the Union Trust Company." *Task Report* to the Dept. of Housing & Development, Fairfield University, 1974
54. ibid. p. 22
55. Youngblood, *op. cit.* p. 78
56. Wiener, *op. cit.* p. 132
57. Halloran, J. D., P. Elliot and G. Murdock: *Demonstrations and Communication: A Case Study*. Penguin, Harmondsworth, 1970
58. ibid.
59. ibid.

BIBLIOGRAPHY

Read, H.: *Art and Society*. Faber & Faber, London, 1967
Unesco: *The Arts and Man*. United Nations Educational, Scientific and Cultural Organization, Paris, 1969
Richards, J. M.: *Modern Architecture*. Pelican, Harmondsworth, 1962
Koestler, A.: *The Act of Creation*. Pan, London, 1969
Gregory, R. L.: *Eye and Brain*. McGraw-Hill, New York, 1973
Tyler, P.: *Sex, Psyche, Etcetera in the Film*. Penguin, Harmondsworth, 1971
Agel, J.: *The Making of Kubrick's 2001*. Signet, New York, 1970
McCauley, C. S.: *Computers and Creativity*. Praeger, New York, 1974
Halas, J.: *Computer Animation*. Focal Press, London, 1974
McLoughlin, J. B.: *Urban and Regional Planning*. Faber and Faber, London, 1970
Misra, R. P.: "The Diffusion of Information in the Context of Development Planning," *Lund Studies in Geography,* 37, 1971, pp. 118-136

2

Towards a socio-semiology of performance

John Andrew Fullard van Zyl *was born in 1934, educated at Grey College and graduated with an M.A. in English at the University of the Orange Free State. He was awarded a Rhodes Scholarship in 1958 and read English Language and Literature at Oxford, receiving an M.A. in 1961. He was awarded a Ph.D. by the University of the Witwatersrand in 1972. Since 1962 he has been on the full-time staff of this University, first with the Department of English and since 1972 with the School of Dramatic Art.*

Introduction

Extending the argument that the illiterate of the future will not be those who cannot read, but those who cannot see, this paper looks at the methods man uses to look in on himself (e.g. theatre, film, TV) and emphasizes the need for a language to analyse social performance. This language has as its broad base, the organization of experience shaped by the purposes of the communicator, the nature of the receiver, the qualities of the event to be communicated and the technology and mechanics of the medium. Theatre, for example, is society studying itself in various mirrors. The images that society sees refracted can make it weep, laugh or come to a revolutionary decision, but always theatre remains an integrated part of society as well as an expression of it. The advent of electronic communication has enabled Youngblood to redefine Jacques' adage, ''All the world's a stage'' to ''The world is not a stage but a TV documentary, and thus through the medium of TV mankind is in direct contact with the human condition, and therefore the need to represent it through art falls away.'' [1] The issues raised by this statement have already been dealt with in Chapter One, but the implication is that electronic technology is far in advance of man's ability to satisfactorily decode and interpret events in society or events transmitted via the media. Where the media not only are capable of changing society, but are also able to redesign our cities the analysis of the content of media assumes a fundamental role if man is to understand and control such changes.

A semiology of performance offers such a methodology.

K.G.T.

1. Youngblood, G.: *Expanded Cinema.* Studio Vista, London, p. 78

Towards a socio-semiology of performance

If the major part of human activity (including the so-called disinterested operations of scientists) can be seen as a type of performance, and if all these performances add up to a form of communication called social discourse, then some sort of decoding mechanism must exist to interpret these performances and to give them meaning.

Discourse implies language, and social discourse is indisputably a language in the broader sense of being an organization of experience shaped by the purposes of the communicator, the nature of the receiver, the quality of the event to be communicated and the technology involved in the functioning of the medium.

Similarly, the idea that all cognition, the process by which man perceives and relates to the world is, ultimately, a matter of language, is basic to structuralism. Almost every phenomenon that occurs in nature or in society, whether it be bees dancing, or the type of clothes worn by a person or the model of car bought, can be read as a statement, a unit of information.

Strictly, structuralism may be defined as a mode of analysis of cultural artefacts which originates in the methods of contemporary linguistics. Linguistics is not only a stimulus and a source of inspiration, but a methodological model, which unifies the diverse projects of structuralists. It boils down to attempts to analyse various practices as languages, or codes. This gives rise to the basic belief that if human actions and productions are to have meaning, there must be an underlying system of distinction and conventions and codes which makes this meaning possible.

Drama, as an artform, exists as a complex set of relations, and lends itself to structural analysis in a particularly significant way. When one studies the system of relations one might be termed a structuralist, and when one studies the signs within the system one might be said to be a semiologist. Obviously, the two critical systems are closely related, and this essay will employ both.

It has long been a commonplace that drama is the most social of all artforms – it must be extended from an individual creative activity into a social creative activity. Thus, in transmission, reception and response, drama operates in an obvious social context. This has been extended into the image of the world as a stage: *teatrum mundi*, of men as actors assuming and discarding different roles, and of the world of social reality being a play contrived by higher forces. This concept of the world as a stage is given direct expression in *As You Like It* through Jacques' speech:

> All the world's a stage,
> And all the men and women merely players.
> They have their exits and their entrances.
> And one man in his time plays many parts.

Over the entrance to the Globe Theatre was the inscription *Totus Mundus Agit Histrionem,* which emphasizes this conception of world-as-stage.

Lately, the social sciences have been appropriating the image and begun using it as a model for analyzing social behaviour. The two siblings of the theatre – film and television – have also played their part in sustaining the image, and it follows that the work of film semiologists like Metz and Eco might be valuable in assessing the relationship between theatre and society.

The most important effect that this application of the linguistic model to theatre has had, is the formulation of the *dramatistic* model. This does not merely use the metaphor or simile of the world being like a stage or standing for a stage, but, instead, uses the metonymic device of stating that the world is a stage. In other words, the dramatistic model is not merely a methodology, but is also an ontology. Social reality, as a system of discourse, can be analyzed by seeing it as a *teatrum mundi* with the concomitant references to such terms as "act", "seem", "character", "performance" and "role". Seeing Hitler as the *villain* of Europe, speaking about the *last act* of the Battle of Stalingrad, and of the *performance* of the troops, can only come from a mind which perceives the events as part of a larger drama.

The ontological implications of Hamlet being unable to act (i.e. undertake significant action) since he cannot "act" (i.e. dissemble, pretend) are much more significant than the metaphorical. When he replies to his mother, "Seems, madam! Nay, it is, I know not 'seems' ", he is in fact enacting his conception of himself and of his situation. Since he gradually begins to realize the double, and contradictory nature of the role he has been called upon to play – that of "scourge" and "minister" – he tries to be "not-himself". He "acts" mad, he "acts" lover, he "acts" playwright so that he need not ACT. It is only when he finally can "act"/ACT in as corrupt a fashion as the Court of Denmark (sending Rosencrantz and Guildenstern to their death, leaping into Ophelia's grave to rant) that he can kill the King and be killed. For Hamlet to stop "acting" is to be corrupted and finally to be damned. His advice to the Players is comparatively simple, "Suit the action to the word, the word to the action", but cannot be applied to his condition since the "word" (the Ghost's injunction) is so much more complex.

Ultimately, Hamlet finds himself in a situation which is untenable since his "acting"/ACTING stands in metonymic relation to the situation. It is part of the situation and stands for the situation. When it changes, the situation changes. The whole structure changes, not just a part of it.

Similarly in *The Tempest* Prospero learns to move from the library to the theatre, from the written word to the enacted word. As the dramatist of the magic island, his Imagination, Ariel, creates storms that do no hurt to man (as scenic effects created by stage-designers are harmless), feasts that appear and disappear, and eventually the momentary triumph of good over evil.

It is only when Prospero breaks his wand and steps outside the role of dramatist that he and the other characters acquire an independent dimension not in metonymic relation to the created world of the island. They then assume the perceiving status that Rosencrantz and Guildenstern have in Stoppard's *Rosencrantz and Guildenstern are Dead*. The freedom they have achieved is far more restricted and dangerous than the more obviously fictional quality of their created roles.

Similar dramatistic models may be applied to Pirandello's *Six Characters in Search of an Author, Troilus and Cressida* and *Twelfth Night*.

A contemporary cinematic analogy with the dramatistic model is to be found in Ingmar Bergman's *Persona*. In this film Bergman has the tragic actress playing Medea lapse into silence in the face of the unstructured (but mediated by technology) tragedy of the television film of the Buddhist monk immolating himself, or the photograph of the little Jewish boy raising his hands in surrender in the Warsaw ghetto. Bergman reminds us, and himself, that technology can render the performances of social life so directly that the traditional form/content or artist/craftsman opposition no longer holds true. The burning Buddhist monk enacts the ultimate role, death, repeatedly as the film is shown repeatedly to an audience that was not even present at the moment of death. How fatuous it seems then to create drama so obviously artificial as a Greek tragedy. Youngblood says that life is no longer a stage, but a television documentary, but Bergman would say that life is both a stage and a television documentary.

Hamlet is both actor and actant, Prospero is both dramatist and character, the unknown television cameraman who filmed the immolation is both artist and technician.

At a performance of radical theatre, the audience is part of the performance and there is no division between stalls and footlights. Signifier and signified become one. In cinema-veritè the characters play themselves and enact their lives before the camera. They create and are created; they all stand in metonymic relation to the completed part. Film and television technology increasingly emphasizes the part-whole relationship of metonymy, as well as the decreasing significance of the either/or alternatives of art/life.

There is a view which sees the dramatistic vision as being merely a metaphor, a heuristic device that helps to clarify the many aspects of social action and interaction. Erving Goffman maintains that men are not really acting out roles in everyday life and that phrases applied to everyday behaviour like "back-stage and frontstage", "performers and audience" and real-life "settings" were only a strategy. "It should be admitted that this attempt to press a mere analogy so far was in part a rhetoric and a manoeuvre."[1]

Goffman is essentially still thinking in metaphoric terms and structural linguists would disagree with his thought that a figure of speech can be used without its relation to the referent being accorded an ontological significance.

A closer look at the metaphor-metonymy distinction may cast more light on the problem. Most literary handbooks define metaphor as any and all substitutions of a figurative word for a literal one in any context, and this is the sense in which it is commonly, and misleadingly, used. Metaphor and its relative, simile, are essentially based on a comparison, or a likeness or an analogy between the referent and the analogue – "ship of the desert" for camel, "canary" for informer, "run like the wind" for speed.

Metonymic substitution, however, is based on an association, an existential link between the literal term and its substitute – "hands" for factory-workers, the "crown" for the government. This distinction is also valid for the subdivisions of metonymy like synecdoche.

Film language has played its role in redefining the distinction between metaphor and metonymy. Indexical signs like a sailor's rolling gait contain an existential link between referent and analogue. The fact that signifier and signified are identical in film would also have contributed to this denotation/connotation relationship.

Jakobsen has not only drawn attention to the fundamental difference between these two figures of speech (or sight) but also to the difference that may be observed in larger patterns of discourse. He has shown how different styles and modes may be distinguished according to the use that is made of either metaphor or metonymy:

"The primacy of the metaphoric process in the literary schools of romantic-ism and symbolism has been repeatedly acknowledged, but it is still insufficiently realized that it is the predominance of metonymy which underlies and actually predetermines the so-called 'realistic' trend."[2]

As most films are essentially "realistic" in style, it is easy to see how difficult it is to sustain a metaphor. Even the much-quoted comparisons between a peacock and Kerensky in Eisenstein's *October* and a spider and the factory-owner in *Strike* seem to be literary rather than cinematic tropes. On the other hand the barren island in Antonioni's *L'Avventura* or the sandpit in *Woman of the Dunes* are directly cinematic and metonymic images.

Jakobsen goes on to suggest further extensions of his distinction into art, Freudian analysis and anthropology. Cubist painting (with its debt to film) is metonymic since the object is dissected into a series of synecdoches. Surrealist art is manifestly metaphorical. Freud's investigation into the structure of dreams resolves itself into whether the symbolism expressed is based on *contiguity* (metonymic "displacement" and synecdochic "conden-sation") or on similarity (metaphoric "identification"). Frazer's taxonomy of magic reveals two types of rites: those based on the law of similarity and those based on the association by contiguity – the former identified as homeopathic magic, the latter as contagious magic. Jakobsen's conclusion that the study, and identification, of metonymy has been neglected in favour of metaphor, because metaphor is found primarily in poetry and most rhetorical criticism has concentrated on poetry rather than the novel, is interesting but is only a partial answer.

It is possible that the metonymic mode itself has assumed a greater significance in contemporary communication and sign-making due to the thoughts of such critics as Kermode in *The Sense of an Ending*, and Brian Wicker in *The Story-Shaped World*. In both of these works the fictiveness of thought is stressed, and the boundaries between art/life are blurred. The more the clear distinction between performer/audience (as in radical theatre), art/life (as in cinema-veritè) and beauty/function (as in the motorcar or most machines) is lost, and the greater the active participation by the viewer/consumer/actor, the more man stands in metonymic relation to the experience that he enacts.

The desire to use the metaphoric rather than the metonymic model seems to represent a desire to reinforce the dualisms that are characteristic of

Western society. Such antinomies as man and nature, mind and body, form and matter and the universal and the particular have always been structured in a horizontal relationship in which the higher is set against the lower, and the lower can never be assimiliated into the higher. The contemporary metonymic view sees the one level as being part of the other, and thereby reduces the two dimensions of man as set out by Marcuse into one.

Due to the binary nature of metaphor, we have to deny the literal truth of an image if we are to understand its metaphorical significance. In Macbeth's speech

> Sleep, that knits up the ravell'd sleeve of care,
> The death of each day's life, sore labour's bath,
> Balm of hurt minds, great Nature's second course . . .

however much one may sympathize with his problems, it is obvious that sleep is neither a bath, nor a needle. The dramatistic vision, however, need not be denied its literal truth before it can be affirmed as an analogical truth.

Structural linguistics again serves to create a link between the analogic/metonymic causal relationship and the paradigmatic structures of linguistic theory. There is a parallel relationship between the metonymic/paradigmatic and the metaphoric/syntagmatic relationships. It was Saussure who first pointed out that the grammar of a language has two major components: an associative, paradigmatic grammar and a syntagmatic. The former is an analysis of relations within a process and operates on a *both-and* basis, and the latter is an analysis of relations in a system and operates on an *either-or* basis.

If man tries to make sense of his experiences by constructing "fictions", whether they be dreams, myths, fairy-tales or dramas, it is first necessary to distinguish between the paradigmatic and the syntagmatic elements. It is essential that this be done so that the metonymic relationship between perceiver and perceived (the paradigmatic) be clearly separated from the metaphoric (or syntagmatic) relationship.

A consideration of cinema as a form of discourse casts further light on the problem of the dramatistic model as a means of analyzing social discourse. If the world is no longer a stage, but a television documentary, one might be forgiven in calling this model the cineastic approach. One of the major problems to be solved is related to the methodology to be used in decoding the theatre and film language – is it to be the analogic or digital form of analysis?

There are basically two kinds of computer systems which may be used as methodological models: those that measure and those that count. The type of computer that *measures* is an analogue computer because it points out analogic connections between the measured quantities and the numerical quantities that represent them. A speedometer, and a thermometer, are examples of basic analogue computers.

A computer that *counts* is called digital because its on/off switches perform direct (not analogic) functions. This system has two as its base, hence it operates on a binary code, in much the same way that metaphor does.

Digital communication is almost always concerned with discrete elements, breaks in continuity and the spaces between units of meaning. It deals with choice and it deals with negatives (the elements of "not" and "either/or") rather than with the more inclusive "both/and", (which relates in its turn to the metonymic model). All linguistic communication which is denotative in form could be considered to be digital. Phonemes which serve to separate out units of meaning within the continuum of sounds that constitutes speech would be digital.

Analogic communication, on the other hand, does not deal with breaks in meaning and constitutes itself in continuous forms of mutating meaning. It is not concerned with "not" or "either/or" sets, but rather with varying pitches, quantities, densities or rhythms. Gestures and movements, dances and film sequences, songs and symphonies are all analogical forms of communication.

Not only are analogic forms usually polysemic in that several sign systems are being utilized at the same time, but it is difficult to isolate any one component without reference to its antecedent and consequent components. Simple-minded image-counting in Shakespeare's plays, based usually only on texts, which come to the conclusion that there are X number of references to monkeys and goats in *Othello* usually ignore the "thickness" of a performance which at any moment exists diachronically and synchronically. Those references to monkeys and goats might be ironic since they are being used anaphorically (referring back to an element previously used) or exorphorically (referring beyond the text at that moment to an independently established reality).

This sort of discourse analysis which deals with any performance as a series of ongoing, mutating elements, places great emphasis on the patterns that emerge in which the unit details are subsumed or even sublimated.

It is an unfortunate fact that an analysis of a play or film is usually cast in the digital mode. This is due to the fact that plays are more often *read* than observed when being analyzed by a critic, and that film criticism has followed dramatic criticism and its conventions until very recently.

When a play is read in text-form, an interpretation must inevitably be word-bound, hence digital. It is only lately that film criticism has, under the influence of semiologists, begun to consider this basic premise and begun to exercise an interactive effect on dramatic analysis. Through this, the work of Birdwhistell on Kinesics has been rediscovered.

A more detailed examination of the language of film reveals it to be a useful model for the analysis of social discourse since it so patently employs an analogic and metonymic approach.

The observations made by the new school of semiotic film critics like Christian Metz, Peter Wollen, Guissepe Bettetini and Umberto Eco all lend strength to this position. Some of the more pertinent conclusions they have come to may be summarized as follows:

1. The main difference between linguistics and the semiology of film lies in the fact that film unlike verbal language lacks double articulation. Unlike language that can with a limited number of phonemes produce an unlimited number of combinations giving rise to unlimited morphemes, film cannot break the shot into smaller components, like the frame, for instance. The conventional nature of the phoneme is missing. *Cat* can be broken into c-a-t, but parts of a shot are isomorphic.

2. The second point is therefore, that in the filmic sign, the signifier and the signified are identical. In its perceptual literalness the image reproduces the signified spectacle whose signifier it is, and then becomes what it shows, to the extent that it no longer has to signify it.
   This is a new issue. In any traditional work of art the world that is represented (the denoted) never constitutes a major part of what the author has to say. In non-representational art, like music, it is even missing. When it is present in literature, its function is only to introduce the expressed world – the connotative level. In the cinema the connotative is linked to the denotative.

3. In linguistics the basic element of analysis is the word. In film it is the shot. The two are qualitatively different. A shot is not a single lexical unit of discourse but a highly complicated record of relations within, and properties of its referent. The shot exhibits these relations within, and properties expressing them in separate lexical units manipulated by syntax. The shot itself is not a single lexical unit in so far as it exhibits an undefined range of meanings which can mutate into each other imperceptibly. A shot of a street does not merely indicate one predicate, i.e. a street, but also that the street is long, cold and dark. Even the most apparently objective of shots is filled with denotations due to the polysemic nature of films.

4. The image is always located in a specific narrative environment. Shots are not words, they are statements. A shot does not simply state street, but *here is the street*. The shot is not only a statement, it is a literal statement, in which both contingency and simultaneity play an important part. One cannot separate the street from its contingent darkness, neither can you separate the man walking down the street from the simultaneous swing of his arms or angle of his chin. There is no equivalent in literature for "getting things in the same shot" in which several actions and objects are related spatially and temporally. The writer must show successively, the cinema can show simultaneously.

5. Peter Wollen has used C. S. Peirce's taxonomy of signs to develop a basic film vocabulary. Peirce divided what he called the second trichotomy of signs into icons, indices and symbols. An icon is a sign which represents its object mainly by its similarity to it, the relationship between signifier and signified is not arbitrary, but one of likeness. An index is a sign by virtue of the existential bond between itself and an object. It operates metonymically–the part being an index to the whole. A symbolic sign requires neither resemblance to its object, nor an existential bond with it, but is conventional and culture-bound. A portrait of a person is an iconic image, the drunken stagger is an index to the state of inebriation of a man, the worker tied to the giant pressure gauge in the factory in *Metropolis* is symbolic of the fate of the labourers in a capitalist society. All three signs must invariably overlap somewhere, since every film image is basically iconic, and then can be indexical or symbolic at a second stage, or even shift from one to the other.

All the points raised finally relate to a basic critical stance first articulated by Pasolini: "A film is stylistic before it is grammatical." By this he means that a film, lying closer to poetry and drama than prose, belongs to analogic communication. Cinema's basis lies with images, dialogue, music and relates to the functions of Freud's unconscious, primary process of decoding. The irrational, hallucinating quality of primary cinematic communication (i.e. the first experience of a film before a critic re-experiences it several times for study purposes) is akin to dream and memories.

The *content* of a film which is often reducible to binary oppositions (as in Kitses' analysis of the Western in which he finds ploughshare/gun, community/individual oppositions) and therefore to digital analysis, may be considered without reference to the style of the director. Since cinematic style must be suppressed to reinforce the contextual reading of a film (or the work of an *auteur*) films are forced into a grammatical mode.

When, however, the flow of sequences, the mutation of images, the gradients of colour and movement are seen within their proper analogic mode, the stylistic and expressive meaning of a film can often be seen to negate the simplistic, grammatical reading.

Performance, whether it be in the theatre or within society, can be examined in the light of the analogic mode of communication as well. The work of Gregory Bateson, E. T. Hall and Ray Birdwhistell in the development of the science of Kinesics – a study of human body motion behaviour based on analogical analysis of gesture, posture, grouping, and constellations of groupings – comes to mind here. Kinesics has been adapted as a methodology for studying analogue behaviour and also for studying performance. As Ruesch and Kees write:

"The principles of analogic codification as contrasted with digital codification have a central importance to students of human behaviour that is still perhaps insufficiently understood. The use of words, whether in speech or writing, has certain limitations, akin to those of digital computers: words remain identifying or typifying symbols that lack the impelling immediacy of analogic devices. Words or a series of words are emergent phenomena that, because of their step characteristics, lack the property of efficiently representing continua or changes over time."[3]

What the passage quoted emphasizes is the continuous gradient of change (mutation) which occurs organically throughout a performance. The metaphor that obtains here is consciously taken from biology whereas the metaphor that obtains for digital analysis is more closely related to electrical engineering: impulses being activated, and circuits being switched on and off. As the study of non-verbal behaviour (images, actions, gestures, even the use of words-as-sounds in opera) Kinesics helps illuminate the interpretation of dramatic texts. As Birdwhistell sees it, dramatic communication is a continuous process conveyed by a polysemic system.

"I have posited communication as a multi-channel system emergent from and regulative of the influenceable multi-sensory activity of living systems. Within such a frame of reference, spoken and body motion languages are infra-communicational systems which are interdependently merged with each other and with other comparable codes utilizing other channels to become communicative."[4]

No one sign system can alone convey meaning, and any attempt to make it do so remains reductive and simplistic. Any attempt to read a film or a play as if they were only the sum of a novelistic plot, character and dialogue, is illustrative of this interpretative method. Meaning must be the sum of the layers of significance that reside in the polysemic mode. Any attempt to decode such a mode (drama, dance, film or social discourse) must take cognizance of the complexity of the cross-referencing and multi-channeled systems.

Some of the infra-systems (channels) would have to rely on cognitive procedures for decoding (montage in film, the use of masks in theatre, salutations or forms of precedence in social discourse). Others would be culturally determined (gesture in Balinese dancing), others again might be related to private behaviour (submitting by lowering the eyes).

At present the means of decoding fictional artefacts, even the sophisticated codes of Roland Barthes (the proairetic, the hermeneutic, cultural, connotative and symbolic), are effective only when dealing with literary texts.

Birdwhistell has used a linguistic model for the notation of movement, and it has the merit of belonging to the analogical mode. His definitions of the smallest particle of visually perceptible motion (the *Kine*), sets of Kines that compose a particular motion *(Kinemorph)* and variations of Kines that do not constitute a change in meaning *(alloKines)* are a useful tool in decoding a major aspect of performance. Noting a change in one of the component Kines can alert an interpreter to a change in any of the other layers of encoding. Contrast-analysis, mirror-relationships, empirical measurement through video-taping and filming are all part of kinesic decoding.

Hopefully this methodology will be extended to other cognate disciplines and will itself be examined more closely as a tool of analogic analysis, especially since the nature of society has been altered so radically by technology. New modes of interpreting and decoding behaviour – whether it be on stage, in film and television, or within the structures of post-modern, neotechnic society – must be found.

As Marcuse has pointed out, two-dimensional man was based on the nature of the opposition of form and matter, mind and body, and the individual and the universal – the traditional conception of man in pre-neotechnic society. What transformed two-dimensional society into one-dimensional was the process of technological mediation, as Gilbert Simondon expresses it:

"One cannot speak of the work of a machine, but only of its function, which is an ordered totality of operations. Form and content, if they still exist, are on the same level, are part of the same system, there is continuity between technology and nature." [5]

The antitheses of the two-dimensional world have been transformed into a convergence of functions, a structural unity, by technology. The machine creates a continuity between machine and man, machine and nature, and man and nature. A self-regulating system has been created with technology providing the mediation through which everything which is outside can be assimilated without doing any injury to the structure. Transformations (allied to the kinesic and the analogic) ensure that the mentonymic quality of all the elements is kept within the system, and the mutations are never reduced to the either/or antitheses of the digital counter. Whether it be international relations or a Republican-Democrat election issue, the harsh dualism of previous historical periods no longer obtains.

This has led to what Shapiro calls the "universal semiotic of technological experience". The technological mediation between the inherent dualisms of Western society has resulted in a semiology in which language and functional sign and symbol system have become integrated. An important feature of this semiology is the blurring of the distinction between the conscious and the unconscious, through the attainability of unconscious desires. Objects such as motorcars are transformed into signs, symbols are manufactured to order, and function and beauty become one. Technology succeeds in deconstructing the unconscious, and then restructuring it in forms that constitute the external world, and the consumer-ethic of the capitalist world facilitates the process. As Mumford puts it: "The integral aesthetic organization of the machine becomes, with the neotechnic economy, the final step in ensuring its efficiency." [6]

The net result of this blending of art and function and the machine and the senses is to make technology a form of sense-experience and experience a form of technology. As Shapiro says: "Just as the technical world and the world of commodities and objects become anthropomorphic, so the human world becomes technomorphic." [7]

It is principally through contemporary design that art and technology have reached the common ground which lends itself to semiotic analysis. The predominance of the visual sense (in photography, colour design, interior decorating, film titles, etc.) has been emphasized and made more intense and in greater volume by technology. Millions of copies of the Mona Lisa have created an art gallery without walls where each man is his own curator. Esoteric films like Bunuel's *Tristana* are seen by audiences of thousands and become common property. Television establishes itself by merely being "there" and rewrites the conception of an audience. The World Cup televised redefines drama. The active participation of the eye of the beholder in Op Art redefines visual art. In an Andy Warhol movie and in a John Cage composition the experience of the work is an active, open-ended act of creation: drag-time and drug-time as Parker Tyler puts it. The act of performance is the act of creation is the act of criticism. The part stands for the whole, is part of the whole and ultimately is the whole.

FOOTNOTES

1. Goffman, E.: *The Presentation of Self in Everyday Life.* Doubleday, Garden City, 1959, p. 254
2. Jakobsen, R: *Fundamentals of Language.* Mouton, The Hague, 1956, pp. 91, 92
3. Ruesch, J.: *Communication.* Norton, New York, 1972, p. 8
4. Birdwhistell, R.: *Kinesics and Content.* University of Philadelphia Press, Philadelphia, 1970, p. 2
5. Simondon, G.: *Du Monde d'Existence des Objects Techniques.* Aubier – Montaigne, Paris, 1958, p. 242
6. Mumford, L.: *Technics and Civilization.* Harcourt, Brace and World, New York, 1963, p. 253
7. Shapiro, J. J. in Breines, P. (ed): *Critical Interruptions.* Herder and Herder, New York, 1976, p. 212

BIBLIOGRAPHY

Burns, E.: *Theatricality.* Longmans, London, 1972
Lyman, S. M. and M. B. Scott.: *The Drama of Social Reality.* O.U.P., New York, 1975
Hawkes, T.: *Shakespeare's Talking Animals.* O.U.P., London 1972
Wicker, B.: *The Story-Shaped World.* Athlone Press, London, 1976
Kermode, F.: *The Sense of an Ending.* O.U.P., London, 1967
Saussure, F. de: *Course in General Linguistics.* McGraw-Hill, New York, 1966
Metz, C.: *Language and Cinema.* Mouton, The Hague, 1974
Metz, C.: *The Language of Film.* O.U.P., New York, 1975
Scholes, R.: *Structuralism in Literature.* Yale University Press, New Haven, 1974
Williams, R.: *Television, Culture and Technology.* Fontana, London, 1974
Schechner, R.: *Public Domain.* Bobbs-Merrill, New York, 1966
Kott, J.: *The Eating of the Gods* Chatto and Windus, London, 1975
Kitses, J.: *Horizons West.* Thames and Hudson, London, 1972
Marcuse, H.: *One Dimensional Man.* Beacon, Boston, 1964
Barthes, R.: *Elements of Semiology.* Jonathan Cape, London, 1968

3

Media and change

Robin Henry Lee was born in 1939, educated at St. John's College and obtained an Honours degree in English at the University of Natal. Subsequently he gained a Ph.D. at the University of the Witwatersrand in 1971. Robin Lee was a lecturer in the Department of English, became Director of the Educational Technology Unit at the University of the Witwatersrand, and he is at present Project Manager of the Urban Foundation.

Introduction

The new media have been traditionally characterized by the thesis of change. Research has pointed to two opposing effects of the media on society. On the one hand the media are capable of a positive contribution to the decision-making mechanisms of society and on the other of abetting manipulation, distortion, confusion and control. The consequences of these dichotomous trends have been succinctly stated by Schwartz: "Unless we extend humanistic ethics into the electronic environment we will have the right to speak, but not to program; the right to assembly, but not to connection, the right to due process, but no way to influence the judgements of computers". [1]

In this chapter Robin Lee argues that often the means, the medium, determine the end, by suggesting ends we never knew before. The advances in computer and telecommunications technology, for example, can provide an infrastructure which could ensure social and economic improvements for both urban and rural citizens in industrialized countries. Robin Lee also presents a second, though less publicized, approach in the study of change in relation to society and the new media. This is the school of empirical observation and statistical measurement which operates within the paradigm of normal scientific research. The author then concentrates upon four allied media/change relationships.

1. Social change wrought by changing styles of communications;
2. social change reflected by changing themes;
3. the notion that media are change; and
4. the opposing view that although technology has an inner dynamic for change, it has an external need for stability, and thus resists change.

49

This chapter discusses the importance and value of the two schools of media research.

K.G.T.

1. Schwartz, B.: *Human Connection and the New Media.* Prentice-Hall, Englewood Cliffs, 1973, p. 2

Media and change

From earliest history, media have shaped and directed human society and the individual consciousness. Man has forever extended himself, through one medium or another other than himself, into the world which is not himself. And, in doing this, he has shaped both the world and himself. The medium of language distinguishes man – by the complexity, depth and fluency of the communication possible – from all other inhabitants of the earth, and is in a large measure the reason for our dominance over all the other inhabitants of the earth. The extensions of our physical strengths and manipulative skills through the media of tools and transport, have provided the infrastructure of the technological society we inhabit today. The extension of information storage, carrying and retrieval through electronics is the basis of the mass communications media which are the real topic of this chapter – since we have to consider not only media, but also change. In talking of media and change we talk then of how we became what we are, what we are, and, especially what we are to *be*.

There are, of course, even in our world an infinity – or, at least an indeterminate number – of media. To the artist, almost any material to hand can become a medium of expression, from egg white to polyurethene, from acrylic paint to – as in Andy Warhol – tins of soup. And this observation brings us to the second strand of the matrix linking media and change: the possibility, indeed the inevitability, that media (or means of expression and communication) do not only reflect change, but are themselves in a perpetual state of change. Man's innovativeness expresses itself in the external world through a continuously changing and varying choice of media, singly or in combinations. In that sense, we might do better to think of media *as* change, than of media *and* change. Kafka metaphorically captured this feeling of transition in his story *Metamorphosis*, in which a young man wakes up one morning to find that he has changed into a monstrous beetle. The story itself is concerned with the psychological and social reactions to this unexpected revolution in his life's style; but, from this story, the philosopher Ernest Gellner has produced a definitive statement of the frame of mind (the mental set, if you like) with which the continually changing world of media should be viewed. In a metaphorical sense, we are all always being changed (and changing ourselves) from one state to another; in Kafka's metaphor from men into beetles, or from beetles into men. Media play a large part in the situation of "transition", which is permanently with us. As Gellner observes: "The (modern) world is correctly perceived not through the vision of men nor (the vision of beetles) but through the *doubts* of men-into-beetles." [1]

That word "doubts" sets the tone of this chapter. In this state of transition, the only possible philosophical position is one of organized doubt, and I intend to create that doubt in you by concentrating upon the conflicting theories, the conflicting empirical evidence, and upon the conflict between the conflicting theory and conflicting empirical observation concerning the effect of mass media in and upon our changing culture.

Before we set off on this process of confusion, however, let us ponder for a while the nature of media and its relation to what we call "change". I have already indicated that there is an infinity of *kinds* of media, of which mass communications media are only a complex and local phenomenon. Now I wish to stress the infinity of the *purposes* and *uses* of media, an infinity which is the more remarkable when we recall the limited channels of communication through which men can express themselves and other men can understand or enter into that communication. The sensory channels are, as far as we now know, limited to five – sight, hearing, touch, taste and smell. What is really amazing is the complexity of information that can be conveyed through one or more of these limited number of channels. And here we enter the definition of the third general role of media in change. Though the sensory channels through which creations can be mediated are limited in number, the nature of media available is infinite, and the nature of media-effects is thus infinite. Media can, have, are and will change society continuously – and in doing so, create a perpetual state of transition in which the only possible philosophic stance is one of doubt, of the acceptance of fictiveness.

Among the infinity of uses of media, and the infinity of possible changes thus wrought on society, I wish to concentrate upon *three* relationships between media and change, which will give shape to the rest of the paper. These three relationships are: firstly, that media can reflect and encourage social change by producing changing *styles* of communications; secondly that media can reflect change in the changing *themes* or content of the message carried by the medium; and thirdly and most important, media are themselves a factor in change – *they* change attitudes, *they* alter perceptions, and – complexity upon complexity – they are very often the only means by which we can observe the social and personal changes in which media themselves have been factors of change.

It is not necessary to give examples of each of these three areas — since the reader will surely be familiar with books or films which have social or personal "change" as their themes or content, he can probably recall major changes in the styles of a communication medium (let us say, the discovery of mathematical perspective techniques in the early Renaissance) which reflected and encouraged a fundamental change in the way in which men saw the world, and mediated their vision of it to others. However, let us investigate the idea of media being a factor in change – and not only a reflection of change. This is in fact the oldest effect of media (to be a change factor in society) – but one which we have continually to rediscover and recognize to be the most potent and once again the newest. I want to stress the point by means of three examples taken from diverse sources, all emphasizing that media – art media *and* communications media – themselves *shape* the future, as much as they reflect or comment on the changes that are occurring as a result of other forces shaping the future. The first is quite an unlikely medium—the cave paintings of Altamira in Spain, perhaps the most famous cave paintings of pre-historic man. At first sight, these would seem to record and reflect the world that those men lived in, and would seem also to record certain skills and certain events, mainly hunting. But the interesting thing is that these paintings are not in the main dwelling areas of the caves, where you might expect them to be if they were narrative recordings of real events, used daily to acculturate the young cave dweller. Actually, these paintings are in the deepest and darkest recesses of the caves, and this has suggested to experts that the painting had a magical (and not a narrative) property for the painters and for the tribes. What is even more interesting is an interpretation that Jacob Bronowski has recently given to these paintings:

"I think that the power that we see expressed (in these paintings) . . . is the power of anticipation: the forward-looking imagination. In these paintings the hunter was made familiar with dangers which he knew he had to face, but to which he had not yet come. When the hunter was brought into the secret dark and the light was suddenly flashed on the pictures, he saw the bison as he would have to face him, he saw the running deer, he saw the turning boar. And he felt alone with them as he would in the hunt. The moment of fear was made present to him . . . The painter had frozen the moment of fear, and the hunter entered it through the painting, as if through an airlock.

"For us, the cave-paintings re-create the hunter's way of life as a glimpse of history: we look through them into the past. But for the hunter . . . they were a peephole into the future: he looked ahead." [2]

The Altamira paintings, then, could have been, for those cavemen, both a representation of reality in style and theme, and a factor in shaping their attitude to a reality that *had* not yet come-to-be. Through that medium they projected themselves into, they confronted the future. The same can be said of modern scientific technology, as it manifests itself in communications media.

The second example concerns media as a shaping factor in social change. An American educational technologist named Glenn Heathers has put the idea in this way: "(Modern scientific technology) is the most dynamic single force in determining the scope of our possible duty . . . because it changes the domain of what we can do, out of which emerges the domain of what we ought to do." [3]

Modern communications media – which are, of course, manifestations of and based upon modern scientific technology – have the *same* power as Heathers attributes to technology. Because they change the whole domain of what and how we communicate, they change the whole domain of what we *ought* to communicate, now and in the future. Technological change is – we have to face it – the current imperative of moral change – and nowhere is this felt more acutely than in the communications media, whether used for broadcast or for educational purposes. We all fervently speak of setting our objectives, and then choosing our means: but often the means, the medium, determines the end, by suggesting ends we never knew before.

These two examples – cave painting and scientific technology – both exhibit, then, a crucial fact about media and change. Media capture and reflect the past and the present: but they also project an image of the future, an image which is potent enough to nerve a man to do what he has to do (kill that bison); and potent enough to alter the moral structure of a society. The relation between media and change is, in this perspective, a dynamic relationship – media are change. There is, however, a third view of modern media; a "yes, but on the other hand . . ." kind of argument. Appropriately enough, the "on the other hand" kind of argument comes from an economist. J. K. Galbraith has created the term "the approved contradiction" to describe this on-the-one-hand-and-on-the-other-hand view of a central cultural tension of our time. He agrees that scientific technology actually institutionalizes change – that technology has, in itself, a dynamic imperative for doing things better and (or, at least) differently. Yet successful scientific technology needs massive initial investment in basic research processes which lead only *eventually* to saleable products. It is long term. Scientific technology, above all, requires stable social and political conditions for its successful functioning. Consequently, he argues, technology has an inner dynamic for *change*, and an external need for *stability*. The result, Galbraith argues, is the approved contradiction of modern life, the situation in which "there is no massive change, but, except as the output of goods increases, all remains as before." [4] Once again, a medium of change – or, more accurately, the scientific technology upon which our modern media are based, shows this "approved contradiction" – this tendency to reflect and sustain things as they are, *and* to project man's mind towards things as they should or might be.

This notion of our culture embodying an "approved contradiction" concerning media and change is helpful in another analytical way. It helps us to understand the two schools of thought that exist concerning the relationship between media and change in our culture at this time. The first is the school of empirical observation and statistical measurement, represented by writers such as Wilbur Schramm, J. D. Halloran, Hilda Himmelweit, Paul Lazarsfeld and William A. Belson. [5] These researchers and writers are concerned with identifying and measuring the effects of media upon large populations – simply stated, they are the sociologists of media. They operate under the paradigm of all scientific research: create an hypothesis, define the variables within the measurements required to validate or invalidate that hypothesis, control as many of these variables as possible (preferably all except one), take the measurements, and validate or invalidate the hypothesis. [6] The hypotheses set up in trying to measure the effect of media in changing people's attitudes have included hypotheses concerning violence, sexuality, sport, schooling, transport, food and the attitude to popping down to the local pub for a drink. An immense amount of valuable and informative data has been gathered on the relation between media (films, books and television) and the audience's changing attitudes; and this might be considered the logical and correct way to go about finding out about media and change. There are, however, two objections to this mode of empirical enquiry.

First let us briefly summarize what the findings of these sociologists of media have been. Broadly, the research findings have confirmed the stable and conservative side of Galbraith's "approved contradiction". The empirical research into changing attitudes as a result of mass media (film and television) has shown that very little change does, in fact, occur in people's attitudes. Mass media are in fact "conservative technologies" – they re-inforce the prevailing social and moral consensus. The core moral attitudes of the audience are not deeply affected, even by prolonged exposure to the media. Some South Africans have been known to sit through ten showings of *Last Tango in Paris* without changing their basic disgust and horror at this sign of depravity. People also negate the potentially innovatory effect of media by "selective watching" – they watch only material that fits their existing attitudes – and they increase the conservative effect by "selective retention" – they remember and internalize only the attitudes they already have. In addition, more sophisticated research has shown that, even when new attitudes are learnt, they remain inactive; they are not, in fact, put into operation in interpersonal relationships, though they will be claimed as new attitudes in response to direct questioning.

On the other hand, there are two areas in which mass media can be shown empirically to have changed attitudes and behaviour. Concerning attitudes, the media are immensely potent in altering an individual's peripheral attitudes, and in *creating* attitudes where none were held before (and as it is one of the main functions of television to continuously introduce audiences to material they had never thought of or seen before, this peripheral effect *can* be powerful). Concerning behaviour, it has been shown that both film and television, in historical sequence, deeply altered social patterns – in simple terms, many people went to the cinema or now watch television instead of doing something else: yet their core moral and social attitudes seem to be relatively unchanged.

This conflicting evidence does, in fact, seem to lead to disturbing conclusions. The empirical information seems to contradict all that was previously maintained concerning the vast effect of media on man's attitude to his past, present and future. We must come back then to the two objections to this form of investigation mentioned initially. These objections are, in my opinion, sufficiently deep to cast into doubt (at least temporarily) the whole field of media sociology. First, as Halloran states: "Although sophisticated social science methods make possible important empirical studies, they may also create the danger that the specific problem under investigation will be shaped by the requirements of method rather than of social relevance." [7]

That is, we must face the possibility that these studies do not produce evidence of change, not because there was no change, but because an inadequate paradigm was used – the system measured, but it measured uninteresting material, or irrelevant material, or the investigation was continued over too short a time.

The second objection is more fundamental. The *notion* of social scientific investigation of media and change on sound statistical grounds is itself an intellectual construct, a concept, and blindness to this has sometimes led such researchers to assume that their information is indisputable fact. All it really is, is information within a given context – and that context is woefully small in the full context of human behaviour. Increasingly, it is becoming clear in the social sciences that inadequate paradigms account for neutral results more often than any other factor. The theory by which the enquiry is governed becomes increasingly important.

It will be recognized that the early sections of this chapter were deeply influenced by the thinking of the major media theorist – Marshall McLuhan. Two points may be made concerning his ideas, points which are typical of media theory as a whole. First, the conceptual structure with which McLuhan approaches media and change is derived from several existing disciplines; primarily, the study of aesthetic effects of media (that is why he is often so illuminating on the role of the artist in change[8]) but also the role of psychology, sociology, history and technology. In this way, he differs markedly from the empirical school. That school has attempted to delimit the effects of media by using paradigms and models derived from *one* discipline – and, as suggested, this is inadequate to the problem. McLuhan's composite approach – though leaving him open to charges of superficiality by *each* of the disciplines – seems to confront the complexity of the interaction of media and change at an altogether more satisfying level.

Secondly, McLuhan has radically shifted our view of media, by being able to consider paint and television, the car and sound waves, amongst others, as media. With this more inclusive view, he has been able to give due weight to the formative influence of the medium itself, and thus made that important step from considering "media-and-. . ." to considering "media-as- . . ." In this direction, surely, lies the answer:

"Until writing was invented, we lived in acoustic space, where all backward peoples still live: boundless, directionless, horizonless, the dark of the mind, the world of emotion, primordial intuition, mafia-ridden. Speech is a social chart of this dark bog.

"Speech structures the abyss of mental and acoustic space, shrouding the race; it is a cosmic, invisible architecture of the human dark.

"In the computer age, speech yields to macrocosmic gesticulation on the direct interface of total cultures. The silent movies began this move.

"Writing turned a spotlight on the high, dim Sierras of speech; writing was the visualization of acoustic space. It lit up the dark.

"A goose quill put an end to talk, abolished mystery, gave us enclosed space and towns, brought roads and armies and bureaucracies. It was the basic metaphor with which the cycle of Civilization began, the step from the dark into the light of the mind. The hand that filled a paper built a city.

"The handwriting is on the celluloid walls of Hollywood; the Age of Writing has passed. We must invent a New Metaphor, restructure our thoughts and feelings. The *new media* are not bridges between man and nature. They are nature." [9]

FOOTNOTES

1. Gellner, E. *Thought and Change*. Weidenfeld and Nicolson, London, 1964, p. 58
2. Bronowski, J.: "The Ascent of Man" in *The Listener,* Vol. 89, No. 2032, May 1973, p. 607
3. Heathers, G.: "Educational Philosophy and Educational Technology" in S. G. Tickton (ed.): To Improve Learning, New York, 1971, p. 105
4. Galbraith, J. K.: *The New Industrial State*. Penguin, Harmondsworth, 1967
5. Belson, W. A.: *The Impact of Television*. Lockwood, London, 1967
6. This is, of course, simplified. See the fuller, definitive explanation in Kuhn, T. S.: *The Structure of Scientific Revolutions*. Chicago Univ. Press, 1970, especially Chapters II and III
7. Halloran, J. D.: *The Effects of Mass Communication*. Leicester Univ. Press, 1971, p. 8
8. McLuhan, M.: *Through the Vanishing Point*. Harper & Row. New York, 1968
9. McLuhan, M.: *Counterblast*. Harcourt, Brace and Jovanovich, London, 1969, pp. 15-14

4

Photography, the change agent

Adolf Veenstra *started his career as a biologist. He then went to London to become a musician. He found it difficult to communicate abstract thoughts aurally and became interested in visual communication. This subject has filled his life. He has worked in industry and in advertising. He now heads the graphic and photographic section of the Educational Technology Unit at Witwatersrand University. He is involved with all aspects of visual communication but specializes in the visual portrayal of abstract data especially to supplement sequential speech to aid the communication process. Photography has always appealed to him as an essential tool in our technological society.*

Introduction

"The art scene today is made up of strong extremes. It may seem strange that while the visual arts are predominantly abstract and certainly not realistic, the film as an art form is not going in the same direction. It has developed many new techniques, but its main concern is still with reality — the nude that has been considered outmoded on canvas is here in all its photographic reality!" [1]

Marshall McLuhan's quote in the conclusion of the last chapter which states the view that the new media are nature must be read against the historical succession principle according to which one medium becomes the content of the next. Increasingly, due to lower costs and higher consumer demand, the new media are being made available to every one. Already millions of people own Super 8 cameras, slide cameras, Instamatics and even video recorders. This process has, according to Youngblood, led to a rebirth of the cottage industry where every individual is able through photographic techniques, to apprehend, capture, generate, transmit, duplicate, replicate, manipulate, store and retrieve audio-visual information. For the first time in history every human now has the ability to capture, preserve and *interpret* those aspects of the living present that are meaningful to him. [2] This statement is based upon the assumption that a high general level of visual literacy exists in modern society, a conclusion questioned by the majority of the authors contributing to this book. Youngblood states, "If art is involved, it's the art of creative living as opposed to passive conditioned response." If this is so, then we must ask why it is that the majority of amateur film-makers are more concerned about technique than content. An overwhelming percentage of their efforts are simply bad copies of mediocre conditioned professional productions. Indeed, many a professional film-maker yearns for the freedom and experimentalism available to the amateur. The difference between the professional and the amateur lies perhaps in the professional's heightened ability to perceive and hence to comprehend the nature of his own reality. The professional understands the properties of the chains which constrain him; the amateur who worships the professional misunderstands the commercial function of the professional's constraints and simply imitates him. Man's consciousness has not caught up with his technology and technology is controlled by people who do understand the nature of things and who thereby are able to manipulate society. To use the words of Adolf Veenstra, "because of its facile ability to make images, photography is predominantly a whore".

In this chapter, Adolf Veenstra deals with the effects of still photography on human beliefs, values and attitudes. He discusses some of photography's scientific applications and touches upon its dehumanizing influences as well. His contrasting opinion with regard to amateur still photography raises some interesting issues with regard to the art status of still versus cine photography. The reasons for this dichotomy are partly technical and partly historical. In contrast to his cine counterpart, the still photographer not only has less complicated equipment and simpler matter to capture, but his objectives tend to differ as well. Still photography has followed the lead of art in that the reason for the photograph is to exhibit it to the public. In fact, in the early history of photography, artists and photographers exhibited side by side. The consequent feedback from visitors and artists has therefore been instrumental in elevating still photography to a higher level than amateur cine photography. The worship of technique over content raises some important implications for the future of creative communication technologies at an individual level.

1. The reborn cottage industry will remain at an industrial level and will struggle to transcend its technique constraints and develop into a potent or even meaningful means of communication or interpretation of reality at an individual or personal level.

2. The semantic problem remains. We will never be able to see through each other's eyes, as asserted by Youngblood, because even within the

celluloid world of cine and still photography alone, individuals are unable to find common ground if technique differs.

3. The emphasis on technique automatically subordinates the importance of content and works against art; technique simply reinforces prevailing attitudes and messages.

4. Although many attempts have been made to establish the common root of all the arts, and though significant progress has occurred, the bewilderment that the individual experiences in assessing and interpreting the diverse and contradictory environment in which he lives, leads him to seek refuge in technique and a superficial understanding of what he has done. The question becomes *how* does one photograph, not *what* or *why* does one photograph?

K.G.T.

1. Rookmaaker, H. R.: *Modern Art and the Death of a Culture.* Inter-Varsity Press, London, 1973, pp. 193-194
2. Youngblood, G.: *Expanded Cinema.* Studio Vista, London, 1970, pp. 128-134

Photography, the change agent

We live in a visual culture. We feel at home in visual space – uniform, continuous and connected. Our other senses are subservient to seeing. Before tasting, food and drink must appeal visually. Musicians must pander to the eye in dress and action. The strings bow in unison. Musical scores must be visually attractive and are even exhibited. Few of us enjoy touching anything we have not first seen. We live in an age when the cult of seeing is increasing and for this photography and its derivation, the moving form must be held largely responsible.

Photography is an extension of a powerful sense and the changed scale it introduces in our visual lives is rivalled only by print.

Its very innovation, even before its potential was understood, showed it to be a change agent. It is almost as if photography was something substantial poured into an insatiable void. Probably the first change it caused was in the visual arts. Not only in the confusion it obviously caused by being a new devil – the devil we don't know – but also in the insecurities it produced in those who felt threatened by it. It also provided a new way of seeing the familiar by intensifying it. It showed things the eye is incapable of seeing, for example, exactly how animals move at speed. This is where photography caused intelligent change – not merely a petulant reaction to an automatic paint box.

Besides the broad change photography has made in our ability to discover reality when our blinkers slip and we become receptive to reality, we can isolate the areas which it has reshaped for us.

Because of its facile ability to make images, photography is predominantly a whore. There is little integrity in the mail order catalogues, and advertisements which are foisted on us by, with rare exception, the brash and inept. It is the medium not the content which makes change and here photography has made change. A prostitute also makes money. One inventor of a photographic process, Daguerre, set the ball rolling in 1837, by offering his patent for 400 000 francs. Ten years later, 100 000 portraits were made in Paris alone, and twenty years later 105 million photographs were produced in Britain.[1]

Photography could now change status, not only of itself but also of people – the people who used it and those they depicted. Photographers have received accolades, fame and notoriety. They have had knighthoods bestowed on them. The human subjects they have photographed for the "glossies" have had their lives transformed. They have in turn influenced the ways of living of those of us who want our lives to reflect something of their glamour. Part of our culture is our striving for immortality and as we do not belong to one of the cultures that think that having our photograph taken abducts our soul, we bask in our image being perpetuated, hopefully for eternity.

With its moving form, the cinema, photography changed many lives. It produced not only crass materialism but a change in concepts and values. It is mainly in this modern art form that photography has fulfilled its duty as an art. And that duty is to disentangle the essential strands of existence from complex reality and to weave these strands into strong, emotionally charged, compelling fabrics while remaining true to itself, the medium, and its time, our time. Besides this, the movies and "glossies" have pushed the personality cult of the platform artist beyond the worship of the celebrity. His private moments are no more, particularly if his platform is political or if her's has footlights.

Photography has lamentably changed our lives by systematizing information in a world where humans are reduced to cyphers. From the passport photograph to microfiles and fiches, photography has now become impersonal. Photography has made itself indispensable in the production of print, the medium which has been, and still is, the most exacting form of visual communication. In an age where the communication industry employs more people than any other, perhaps we should note that the speed of technology is always underestimated. Very soon photography will have served its intermediate soulless function as a mechanical recording device and its place will be taken by more efficient machines. Semiconductor, C.c.d. and crystal technology is potentially superior for information storage and retrieval.

In the scientific world photography is not only an essential tool; it is also frequently the end product. Here more than ever the medium has changed the scale which it introduced. Most sciences use photography as an essential tool to achieve an end. Sometimes photography is the end product itself. For instance in fluorescence microscopy and electron microscopy the specimen itself is destroyed and the photograph is the only evidence of the experiment.

The reason for the impact photography has on our lives lies not so much with the camera-wielding protagonist but with the two main attributes of the medium itself.

Firstly, the camera does not lie. No matter how the final image is estranged from the original we believe its message. We remain aware of the relationship between the original and the image. Here we have something magical. We have a communication between the conscious and the subconscious. Surrealistically we give the subconscious a look at the outside world on its own terms and we communicate with the conscious through the idiom of reason.

Photography is part of the industrial revolution, a revolution in which new science and technology are approached with obsolete practices and old ideologies. But in slowly shedding these anachronisms of thought, we have adjusted to change by visually rediscovering the elements of existence.

Thus photography's second major quality becomes evident: it has no thought to the future or hankering for the past. Yet it is in the future that photography must bear witness to the past. It records the immediate now.

This is its primary strength – having the role of not only an historian but also a social conscience. It helps bridge the gap between the ideological potential and the actual realization. In a world where nearly everyone is photographically literate and where photographs have a universal audience on a scale rivalled only by music in its various guises, photography gives us a global language. Not only this, but photography is practised by an amazing number of people everywhere. Many millions of photographs are taken everywhere in the world, by ordinary people who need do no more than decide what they want to record and when to record it. The technology does the necessary to produce the slides and prints which abound in our lives. In Western Germany alone during 1976, 500 million photographs were processed by commercial houses in one year.[2] This figure will not include the clickings of visitors to the country or the goings-on in kitchens or professional studios. This voracious consumer community has created an industry which, with its research, production and marketing, is vast. Photography has become part of our lives. It can make the stark reality of a Vietnamese war orphan's predicament into a reality which can be understood by an empathetic American. Now photography can make change by changing public opinion. A great deal of public opposition to the Vietnamese war can be attributed to photography.

There is also a significant group of dilettantes, the amateurs, who lavish love on what at first seems an effort to keep exhibitions from oblivion, but who provide the enriching points by experimentation and trial which expand our techniques and help photography find its own laws. It is these people who not only record reality but also enable us to discover reality. I suspect it is this group, and the professional in the rare moments of integrity when he becomes an amateur, who will hold off the dreaded moment when photography's working rules become frozen into dogmas.

It is significant that, even in the relatively short existence of photography in relation to our long and vigorous culture, it has become a primary visual force.

FOOTNOTES

1. Scharf, A.: *Art and Photography.* Penguin, Harmondsworth, 1968, pp. 20-21
2. "So Many Photos – So Few Pictures", *Leica Fotographie,* 1976, No. 6, p. 262

5

Telecommunications media and the city

Nick Patricios, *gained his B.Arch at the University of the Witwatersrand in 1972, Diploma of Town Planning and City Planning at the University of Manchester in 1965, and his Ph.D in Town Planning at the University of London in 1970. He presently holds the position of Professor, Dept. of Town and Regional Planning, University of the Witwatersrand.*

Introduction

The concept of communications is analysed in relation to urban structure and form, in terms of channels, networks and terminals or nodes. This chapter shows that the increasing use of telecommunications is likely to lead to a radical change in urban structure and form as understood today and will probably take the form of a spatial reorganization of land uses and nodes. In addition further developments in channel and network technology will no doubt lead to changes in life-styles – schooling, shopping, working, leisure and other activities – with concomitant changes to the urban fabric. Cities enhance communication, and modern telecommunications systems provide the means for extending the web of urban communication beyond geographic boundaries. The concept of "city" in the 21st century is thus likely to have a largely aspatial dimension.

    Many of the processes which may ultimately lead to the kind of society envisaged in Chapter 8, which Peter Goldmark and his associates have termed "The New Rural Society" will be mentioned here. The consequences of new communications technologies discussed in this chapter are important also for the New Rural Society. Since media are playing a growing role in accelerating the rate of social change and if we accept Robin Lee's contentions that "media are change" and that they "are potent enough to alter the moral structure of society" the question becomes: is man capable of handling such change? To what extent will the future impact of new media be determined by rational human decision and be acceptable to society? As in the New Rural Society Project the decisions of today will affect the environment and design of tomorrow. Today man has the ability to make choices for tomorrow to avoid subservience to his machines in the future.

Keyan Tomaselli's conclusions in the first chapter point, however, to man's low levels of visual literacy and his consequent difficulties in understanding and interpreting the content of media. Wilfred Mallows in dealing with city communications systems concurs, "I have a suspicion that our technology has outrun our mental capacity to handle its wider, human repercussions".

Many pop sociologists and science fiction writers have applied their "psychedelic electric kool-aid acid test kits" to this problem. Much man-machine communication has ensued. Numerous conversations between computer programmers, information and video freaks, paleocybernetic man and technological artists with fourth generation intuitive thinking computers, interaction with computer generated holographic images and various other multiple projection electronic machine induced technological vortex environments which integrate multi-channel ideas and messages (as Youngblood and Fuller might say) in a total bombardment of man's visual, auditory and sensual mechanisms do not, however, suggest solutions to the concomitant problems which will face *homo sapiens* in the future. The almost reckless plunge into the metaphysical via the routes of art and technology by writers such as Youngblood[1] and Buckminster Fuller[2], *Total Effect*[3] and many others, and the importance that they attribute to such explorations in their efforts to chart the dawn of man through expanded consciousness devolves upon what Wilfred Mallows has termed the biological ceiling. That is, in each society only a number of people are produced every generation who are capable of handling the problems of a mass production, mass consumption, mass communication society. Without recourse to genetic engineering, it is unlikely that the Youngblood Fuller paleocybernetic consciousness will ever occur for the whole of mankind.

The challenge to urban scientists however, remains a pragmatic one. New communications technologies must assist society to develop in a humanistic direction, must revitalize communities and democracy. Implicit in the successful implementation of these technologies is an acknowledge-ment that the trust and confidence of the subjects in the integrity and responsibility of the system's users is paramount. The use of sophisticated communications technologies without a universally accepted ethical pro-cedure will imprison man in an electronic straitjacket and prevent him or his consciousness from developing to even a fraction of his potential – physically, psychologically or spiritually.

In the year 5555
Your arms are hanging limp
at your sides,
Your legs got nothing to do,
Some machine's doing that for you.

(From "In the Year 2525")

K.G.T.

1. Youngblood, G.: *Expanded Cinema.* Studio Vista, London, 1970
2. See for example, Buckminster Fuller, P.: *Utopia or Oblivion.* Pelican Books, Harmondsworth, 1972 and "Vertical is to Live Horizontal is to Die," *Architectural Design,* Vol. 39., No. 12, 1969
3. Total Effect (L. Allison, L. Jenkin & R. Perrault (eds.)): *Survival Printout.* Vintage Books, New York, 1973

Telecommunications media and the city

In a special edition of *Scientific American* communication is described as the "essence of being human" and also "a vital property of life".[2] Furthermore *telecommunications* media provide "a means of extending the web of urban communication and improving the quality of urban life".[3]

This chapter will consider the ways in which technological advances in telecommunications media influence the city, specifically its physical space and peoples' life styles. A useful conceptual framework for undertaking this is to consider first communication in terms of information theory.

Information theory

The study of communication was greatly advanced by the publication of three works: Claude E. Shannon's paper on "The mathematical theory of communication"[4]; Norbert Wiener's book *Cybernetics: Control and Communication in the Animal and the Machine*[5]; and *Syntactic Structures* by Noam Chomsky.[6]

Shannon's contribution was the establishment of a universal model of communication systems. The elements of his symbolic model consist of an information source, a transmitter, a communication channel, a noise source which is an unpredictable interfering signal that alters or mutilates the desired signal, a receiver, and a message destination. These six elements constitute the basis of any communication system, however complex.

In addition Shannon was able to quantify both the information rate of a message source (a speaker, a person writing, the output of a television camera) and the capacity of communication channels by introducing a measuring unit called a *bit*. A bit (from "binary digit") is a unit of uncertainty or choice; the uncertainty between "yes" or "no" when both are equally likely, or the choice we exercise in selecting unpredictably "left" or "right". The numbers 0 and 1 can specify yes or no, left or right. The bits per message or bits per second establish a measure of the complexity of message sources and the capabilities of channels (Table 1).

One of Wiener's prime concepts is *homeostasis:* the functioning of a system so as to correct adverse disturbances through the detection of deviation from the desired state, and correction by negative feedback. Cybernetics itself is a method of dealing with entropy in systems, whether communications systems or otherwise, by routing information through the necessary channels to maintain homeostasis (or stability). Successful control of information, or cybernetics, is important for, as Wiener states, man is a bundle of decreasing entropy in a world of increasing entropy.

TABLE 1: Capacity of various communication channels
(adapted from table by Pierce, J. R., "Communication", *Scientific American* (227-3), 1972, p.33)

Channel	Capacity in bits per second
Telephone wire (speech)	60 000
AM radio	80 000
FM radio	250 000
High fidelity tape	250 000
Microwave relay system (1 200 telephone channels)	72 million
Commercial television	90 million
L-5 Coaxial cable (10 800 telephone channels)	648 million
Proposed millimetre-waveguide (25 000 telephone channels)	15 billion
Hypothetical laser	100 billion

Shannon's and Wiener's theories were further developed by Warren Weaver[7], W. Ross Ashby[8], and John von Neumann[9]. Chomsky's work led to one important implication for information theory – that of meaning in communication. As Pierce[10] points out the need for communication arises because something "unguessable" must be imparted concerning our understanding or actions. A little must be added to existing knowledge or as a basis for modifying what we would otherwise do. The element of the "unguessable" is what Shannon measures as entropy but the existence of meaning, what we have in *common*, is what reduces it and improves the effectiveness and quality of communication. Yet if we had everything in common little or no communication would be needed. Pierce's contention, by implication, is that communication is not necessary when there is perfect understanding, which is true, but he ignores man's inquisitiveness and curiosity which he attempts to satisfy to a certain extent through obtaining more or new information.

Communities of Interest

The city can be seen as a large information-processing system in which much of the activities involve obtaining, processing and exchanging information. The communication aim, therefore, is to improve the city's capacity to move information rather than people and materials[11]. Meier's book *Communications Theory of Urban Growth*[12] is significant in this respect as he stimulated the development of conceptualizing the city as the focus of *transactions* which he proposed should be measured in information "bits" rather than space. Unfortunately this work still remains at its theoretical stage and little if any empirical research has been undertaken to measure transactions in cities.

The concept of cities in terms of communication transactions is a radical change from the traditional concept of cities as territorial or spatial phenomena. As Webber[13] indicates, if a city is seen as a culturally determined system of dynamic inter-relationships, urban places – such as the central business district, the neighbourhood – should be discarded as concepts. In fact nine factors have been identified by Gottman[14] as to why transactions in quarternary activities would not take place in the traditional central business district.

The non-place urban realm, the community of interest, becomes the framework for human communication. There are countless communities of interest (music, sports, riding, books, politics, etc.) with individuals members of many of them. Within each community of interest people think, act and communicate toward or away from what they, in common, regard as appropriate. As Pierce[15] put it, in terms of information theory only certain messages among all possible messages occur in communication with a community of interest as only certain messages have meaning and will be understood.

If cities are seen as transaction-maximizing systems[16] then the purpose of city planning becomes the promotion of harmonious interaction of the population. Information theory is useful in this context as the vitality of the city can be measured in terms of transactions per unit of time. Thus Meier[17] defines the city as a system which "is a sequence of states of an interacting population, each state being a function of preceding states". The elements of the system are the names and addresses of individual humans and their organizations. The transactions between unitary elements are these messages and movements transmitted through channels, for example, the telephone, radio, television, speech, gesture, pictures, and printed symbols.

Meier's hypothesis is that the transmission of messages creates bonds between people and can be quantified. The more rapidly messages are exchanged the stronger the bond between two individuals or groups becomes. The more internal communication there is in a city, the stronger the "urban bond", which is a function of interaction frequency and distance.

Telecommunications Media

Pierce[18] presents some interesting data on the rise and fall and accelerating use of various media in the U.S.A. The telegraph reached two peaks, first in 1929 and then in 1943, before falling off dramatically after 1960. The increasing use of the postal service and particularly the telephone (Table 2) has contributed to the decline in telegraphy.

TABLE 2: Current rates of increase of mail and telephone calls in the USA (Adapted from Pierce, op. cit., p. 37)

Telecommunications Medium	*Approx. rate of increase per annum*
Pieces of mail per person	3,5%
Local telephone calls per person	5,0%
Toll telephone calls per person	10,0%
Overseas calls per person	25,0%

The publication of new books and new editions of old books rose from about 6 000 per year to a plateau of 12 000 per year during the 1950s which in turn gave way to a steep rise of over 30 000 per year about 1967. Interestingly enough the number of periodicals published in the U.S.A. over the period 1950-1970 increased steadily, whereas the number of newspapers published over the same period has become fairly stable. However it is radio and television which have shown the ascendancy of mass communications media. Whereas virtually every home in the U.S.A. now has both a radio and a television set, the number of radio and television *stations* is still rising.

According to Whyte[19] the telephone and telex services, despite the great impact they have had in shaping the course of industrialized countries, are relatively simple telecommunications media by comparison with those that are now envisaged. Two particular features of the new era will be the emergence of data communications for man-machine and machine-machine telecommunications and a demand for visual telecommunications. In the United Kingdom data transmission services were first introduced in 1965 and the rate of growth still continues at about 100% per annum; there are more data terminals in use in the U.K. today than in the *whole* of the rest of Europe[20]. The 6 000 terminals in use now could well reach over 1 000 000 by the end of the century. As far as image transmission systems are concerned, a whole class of services, including video conference facilities (Confravision), audio-visual educational systems and picturephone, are already in evidence.

The various existing and new telecommunication systems depict what can be described as the *wired city*. The promise of cable television could well produce a fully "wired nation" with voting, shopping, learning, and much of our work being done over multiple cable channels. However, the way cable television has been thwarted in the U.S.A. until the present has been reviewed recently by Godschalk and Merriam[21]. The promise of cable television systems is that they would take over the task of distributing information in bulk from sources to offices and homes. As Goldmark[22] sees it, these systems would be an alternative way of receiving the information that now comes through books, records, broadcasting and so on. As a broad-band, *two-way* information pipe, with a capacity equivalent to 30 or more television channels, the network could be arranged for polling, making requests or seeking information from public institutions.

Implications for urban structure and form

The establishment conception that the media – film, radio and television – simply conduct information has been seriously challenged by Harold Innis[23] and Marshall McLuhan[24]. They have both concentrated on the *forms* of media as the key to the ways in which they have reshaped cultures and personalities[25], on the idea that a *medium* shapes us more thoroughly than its content.

Thus the impact of telecommunication media on people and their activities must not be considered only in terms of information (i.e. the content, quantified or not) conveyed, but on how each medium shapes and influences the information, and ultimately the culture. If one assumes that the medium modifies its content then the media become one of the technological environments of man along with those of production and movement. However the telecommunications media are characterized by the electronic technology of the twentieth century. As Kuhns[26] shows, the crucial differences between the electronic technologies and the mechanical technologies developed in the nineteenth century and carried into this century, are firstly a drastic new form of energy (electricity is mobile energy, unlike steam, wind or water power) and secondly, a different purpose, that of information movement and control (such as the telephone, the telegraph, radio, television and the computer).

Mechanical technology has defined environments in terms of force and its impact historically has been through the energy it has made available, and its ability to take on new kinds of work. On the other hand the electronic media have, for Innis, defined environments largely through the temporal or spatial patterns a new medium makes among the various agencies in the culture; for McLuhan it means ''hot'' or ''cool'', individualizing or tribalizing[27]. McLuhan goes further to suggest that a primary medium shapes the perceptual world of a people, of our awareness of what is outside us.

A fundamental question thus needs to be asked: what influence will telecommunications media as technological environments have firstly on the spatial dimensions of cities, and secondly on the life-styles of people? Before the advent of the electronic technologies the closer individuals were spatially, the greater the likelihood that messages would be transmitted between them. Thus human clustering in cities was a function of distance – but how far will the electronic media in future substitute communications for travel?

Urban structure and forms

Traditionally most interaction between people only took place in a *place*, in spatial proximity to one another. With the introduction of the telegraph and subsequent telecommunications media interaction is increasingly transcending place. The implications of this for urban structure and form have been expounded by Webber[28]. He discusses how spatially dispersed communication between people through electrical communication channels is leading to a non-nodal type of urban structure. The idea of a social community needing to have the propinquity aspect of ''place'', that is, to occupy the same space, is becoming less and less important. Webber redefines communities then as comprising people with common interests who *communicate* with each other; he points out the words community and communication share the Latin root *communis* – ''in common''. Spatial domains become of less significance to interest groups as in modern cities members of various societies, clubs, associations and so on do not come from the same local area. Interests are not related to place although interactions *may* occur in a place.

Webber sees place-related communities becoming less and less significant compared to non-place communities. These interest-communities he refers to as realms which can be conceived as a hierarchy from the world realm, the nation realm, the sub-nation realm, the metropolitan realm, the urban realm, and the local realm. Membership of a realm depends on the level of specialization of the interest: the most specialized people are participants in interest-communities that span the entire world; less specialized people seldom communicate with people outside the nation but interact within it; others seldom directly communicate with anyone outside their metropolitan or urban settlement; and others communicate exclusively with their neighbours in their local realm.

But Webber ignores the psychological need for direct face-to-face contact in interaction and the state of development in telecommunications media. There is no doubt that certain interactions require people to be in the same place in addition to which face-to-face contact can maximize the transaction rate. As Whyte[29] notes, the telegraph and telephone had insufficient decentralizing influence to offset the more powerful centralizing influence of direct face-to-face communication. There is some doubt whether new telecommunications media (video-phones, fast document transmission, etc.) will have sufficient power to offset this centralizing influence. The media do not appear to be at the stage of development where they will provide access for the majority of a population, even in the U.S.A., to two-way visual communication channels with enough capacity in order to substitute for spatial propinquity. Thus the advent of a completely non-nodal and dispersed form of city does not appear to be realizable in this century. However, decentralization of activities will no doubt continue as automatic equipment for transmitting messages increases in use, and as routine and less important transactions are undertaken by computers.

On the other hand, the "aspatial form of city" could become a reality depending on the costs, development and widespread use of cable television and satellites. The latter, it has been claimed by McHale[30], will not only "speed up" communication, but will obliterate the traditional concept of distance. Linking a cable system to a centrally located digital computer could provide for many opportunities, including:

1. channels for groups with special communicative needs, such as doctors and public officials;
2. enable subscribers to order products;
3. enable viewers to take part in public-opinion polls, with the responder's identity concealed if that is desirable;
4. offer educational channels with an option for response by the student; and
5. provide copies of printed material in the subscriber's home.

If the above opportunities were fully utilized, the need for consulting rooms, municipal offices, shops, schools and educational institutions, and libraries would be much diminished if not actually unnecessary.[31]

Life styles

The influence of developments in telecommunications media can be seen in a number of areas of people's lives: education, shopping, health, transportation, and public participation. Much of the information of this section is drawn from Custerson[32] and Goldmark[33]. The latter was chairman of a panel on urban communications established by the U.S. National Academy of Engineering. Their report, *Communications Technology for Urban Improvement*, was undertaken at the request of a number of Federal agencies which sought advice on, mainly, the possibilities of better application of telecommunications technology to city functions in order to improve city living.

In primary schooling the gathering of schoolchildren in a place, the school, represents an important stage in their human-to-human and human-to-object communications. The techniques employed involve improving communication with other children, with play objects and teaching aids and seem to be of uniquely important quality totally insusceptible to telecommunications. The direct human communications process is essential to primary education, thus making necessary the provision of primary schools within close proximity to children's homes. Electronic aids do have their application, but this is best left within the school rather than the home.

In secondary schooling the acquisition of knowledge is of paramount importance and therefore the assembly of school children in one adapted space can be considered unnecessary if telecommunication links are fully established. These would include closed circuit television (CCTV), programmed learning through computer-aided instruction (CAI), and remote access to libraries via computer terminals introduced into the home. Total dispersal of secondary education to the home however may be undesirable as some forms of human-to-human and human-to-object (practical work in science laboratories, etc.) communications are still desirable.

In higher education the same principles that apply to secondary education are relevant. Given maximum telecommunications facilities, including audio-visual return channels to allow for discussion and opportunities to ask questions, a large amount of study could be "remote based". But practical work and the undoubted desirability of social communications on a direct human-to-human basis would ensure the continued existence of some form of adapted space. Of interest would be the physical form of institutions of higher education that would be required, reflecting their new role. Home video shopping could be achieved with goods displayed to the consumer on a viewing screen and orders given by using, say, a simple key board. Packaging and invoicing would take place simultaneously at the warehouse with an automatic debiting of the consumer's bank account. The physical delivery of the chosen goods will depend on the type and size of goods, for if costs allowed this it could take the form of delivery through pneumatic tubes from the warehouse to individual homes or to a local collection point. As the basis for home shopping lies in saving time and energy in travelling, delivery of goods would require some form of automatic distribution. However the value consumers put on human-to-human communications in shopping is not well established, nor that of the desire for social gathering at shopping centres. The impact on the life style of housewives could be dramatically altered with the full establishment of home video shopping. It would certainly be of physical benefit to the less mobile and the elderly and, arguably, to the busy housewife who could transfer the time saved by the use of telecommunications to other outlets.

In the health field the problems of limited numbers of doctors or their uneven geographical distribution could be overcome through telecommunications. One scheme would be to link a doctor by various electronic media to a number of satellite clinics staffed by nurses and para-medical assistants. A television link could be used to obtain an adequate medical history, perform a significant part of the physical examination, read electrocardiograms, examine X-ray plates and so on. Computers could be extensively involved in data collection and could aid diagnosis. Also telecommunication, by its potentiality for reducing travel, may contribute towards the reduction of air pollution and noise from various transport media.

In the transportation field telecommunications are being used to monitor and guide the flow of traffic and to improve the efficiency of mass-transit systems. However the introduction of a system that provides information at every bus stop about routes, frequencies, transfer points, current passenger load and the estimated time of arrival of the next bus would be a great boon in metropolitan areas. On the other hand effective forms of telecommunications associated with terminals and other facilities at home could change people's journey-to-work patterns by diminishing the need for large office concentrations and at the same time alleviate the commuter travel problem.

Finally in the area of public participation, telecommunications, particularly cable television, would assist in increasing the dissemination of information and have an impact on the planning process itself. The increase in the number of channels of communication between officials and citizens can but improve municipal administration. Newspapers, radio and television do not provide for extensive feedback from the public about local matters of concern or about city projects in general. Two-way information flow through cable television has the potential to overcome the present communication gap between officials and the public. A first step would be for the establishment of several community information centres that would tell any caller where to go or call to obtain the information or service requested.

Conclusion

It would be most fitting to conclude on the influence of telecommunications media on people's life style and the structure and form of cities with the implications of Wiener's book *The Human Use of Human Beings*[34]. Wiener considers the computer an advantage in technological terms but at the same time is concerned with possible consequences. He does not seem to fear its dehumanization threat but rather the problem of controlling the machine. If man does not carefully analyze the likely consequences of widespread use of the computer, and by implication other telecommunications media should be included here, he may become subservient to his electronic machines.

One of the possible consequences has been pointed out by Kuhns[35]. Radio, television and films as new forms of leisure have served to intensify man's relationship to the machine, and through their reproduced images and sounds, further separated man from his natural environment. The quality of human life, the style of life have been reshaped by these media. However, the outcome of the extensive use of telecommunications in future, in education, shopping, health, movement, entertainment etc., could create "a curious, and unnatural, form of isolation whose social consequences are difficult to foresee"[36]. It would appear that we must give priority to our value judgement that gives dominance to the human element in the extensive application of any telecommunications media. It is difficult to foresee a situation where most urban activities would be home based in a non-nodal city structure when man's essential biological characteristic is that of gregariousness.

The control of the means of communication thus becomes a vital issue. Gerbner[37] suggests that "any message system produced by an institutional source has certain ideological orientations implicit in selection, emphasis and treatment". Can the mass media be trusted to present an acceptable picture of an overall community of interest? Is it actually possible to do this? Whose interests should be taken into account? Does an overall community of interest exist? These are political and social questions as to the control over the effects of communications.

76   *Nick Patricios*

FOOTNOTES

1. "Communication." *Scientific American,* September 1972, 227 (3), pp. 30-170
2. Pierce, J. R.: "Communication." *Scientific American,* September 1972, 227 (3), p. 30
3. Goldmark, P. C.: "Communication and the Community." *Scientific American,* September 1972, 227 (3), p. 142
4. Shannon, C. E.: "The Mathematical Theory of Communications." *Bell System Technical Journal,* July and October 1948. Reprinted in book form with exposition and comment by Warren Weaver. Urbana, The University of Illinois Press, 1959
5. Wiener, N.: *Cybernetics: Control and Communication in the Animal and the Machine.* John Wiley & Sons, Cambridge, Mass., 1948
6. Chomsky, N.: *Syntactic Structures.* Mouton, Gravenhage, 1957 (8th printing, 1969)
7. Weaver, W. and C. E. Shannon: op. cit.
8. Ashby, W. R.: *An Introduction to Cybernetics.* Chapman and Hall, London, 1956
9. Neumann, J. von (with O. Morgenstern): *Theory of Games and Economic Behaviour.* Princeton University Press, Princeton, 1944; *The Computer and the Brain.* Yale University Press, New Haven, Conn., 1958
10. Pierce, J. R.: op. cit., p. 36
11. Goldmark, P. C.: op. cit., p. 145
12. Meier, R. L.: *Communications Theory of Urban Growth.* M.I.T., Cambridge, Mass., 1962
13. Webber, M. M.: "The Urban Place and the Non-Place Urban Realm," Webber, M. M. *et al., Explorations Into Urban Structures.* University of Pennsylvania Press, Philadelphia, p. 184, 1967
14. Gottman, J.: "Urban Centrality and the Interweaving of Quaternary Activities." Bell, G. and J. Tyrwhitt, (eds.) *Human Identity in the Urban Environment.* Penguin, Harmondsworth, p. 509, 1972
15. Pierce, J. R.: op. cit., p. 38
16. Meier, R. L.: "The Metropolis as a Transaction-Maximizing System." *Daedalus.* Fall 1968, 97 (4), pp. 1292-1313
17. Meier, R. L.: op. cit., p. 2
18. Pierce, J. R.: op. cit., p. 37
19. Whyté, J. S.: "The Impact of Telecommunications on Town Planning." Blowers A, C. Hamnett and P. Sarre (eds.) *The Future of Cities.* Hutchinson, London, 1974, p. 86
20. Ibid., p. 87
21. Godschalk, D. R. and D. H. Merriam: "Cable Television and the FCC: a Crisis in Media Control," LeDuc D. R.: "The Cable Fable," Heitler, B. and Kalba, K. (eds.), *American Institute of Planners Journal,* July 1974, 40 (4), pp. 293-295
22. Goldmark, P. C.: op. cit., p. 145
23. Innis, H. A.: *The Basis of Communication.* University of Toronto Press, Toronto, 1951
24. McLuhan, M.: *The Gutenberg Galaxy.* University of Toronto Press, Toronto, 1962 *Understanding Media: the Extensions of Man.* McGraw-Hill, New York, 1965
25. Kuhns, W.: *The Post-Industrial Prophets: Interpretations of Technology.* Harper Colophon, New York, 1973, p. 132
26. Ibid., p. 117
27. Ibid., p. 121
28. Webber, M. M.: op. cit., p. 96 ff.
29. Whyte, J. S.: op. cit., p. 92
30. McHale, J.: *The Future of the Future.* George Braziller, New York, 1969
31. Goldmark, P. C.: op. cit., p. 145
32. Custerson, A.: (a) "Telecommunications: the Key to the Non-City?" *Built Environment,* July 1973, 2 (7), pp. 403-406. (b) "Telecommunications: Education and Shopping." *Built Environment,* September 1973, 2 (9), pp. 515-518. (c) "Telecommunications: the Office Node". *Built Environment,* November 1973, 2 (11), pp. 647-649

33. Goldmark, P. C.: op. cit., pp. 143-150
34. Wiener, N.: *The Human Use of Human Beings*. Doubleday, Garden City, N.Y., 1954
35. Kuhns, W.: op. cit., p. 100
36. Whyte, J. S.: op. cit., p. 91
37. Gerbner, G.: "Communications and Social Environment." *Scientific American,* September 1972, 227 (3), pp. 153-160

6

A bionic model of society

Melvyn Cunningham Siff *was born in Johannesburg in 1943. He graduated from the University of the Witwatersrand with a B. Sc. in Physics and Applied Mathematics. He obtained his B. Sc. (Hons.) in Applied Mathematics at the same University and at present is completing his M. Sc. in Applied Mathematics on a topic involving mathematical models of brain activity. He has been on the staff of the University of the Witwatersrand for more than 10 years in a variety of fields including Physics, Mathematics and Communications. At present he is a Senior Tutor on the staff of the Communication Studies Department at this University.*

Introduction

Rooting his analysis in neurophysiological principles, Melvyn Siff complements, on a behavioural level, the physical attributes of the communications systems outlined by Mallows in Chapter 7. Whereas Mallows deals with the inadequacies of man's brain and the consequent chaos he has projected onto his externalized model of the brain, the city, this chapter argues that the mental development of any society is subject not only to the limitations of his brain, but also to the richness of man's internal neural and external technological communication networks. The neurosciences, as Mallows has indicated, contain untapped potential in their application in the solution and prediction of existing and future problems in communication research. Traditionally, the neurosciences have been located at a position between philosophy and the psychological-behavioural sciences, and aim to explain the mind/brain and mind/brain/body relationships. Melvyn Siff extends this thesis and develops a bionic model of society by the application of the knowledge of living systems in the management of social processes. The living systems referred to in this chapter should not be confused with the deterministic postulates of Robert Ardrey or the controversial theories of the sociobiologists, but they are rather based on the operation of the human brain to create a synergistic global communications system. Ardrey identifies society as a subconscious model of animal behaviour whereas both Mallows and Siff regard society as a model of man's physiological and particularly, his neurological functions. Because man is most familiar with himself, he has modelled his society on his inner systems. Society may be likened to a child growing up through various stages of development, a million years of human civilization compressed into the twenty years between the emergence of foetal life and maturity. Violence, in terms of Mallows' thesis for example, may be explained as a preprogrammed behaviour pattern, like a printed circuit, inherited from the process of evolution. Once man had developed his third brain, the new mammalian, the inexorable need for violence abated. The printed circuit which caused violence and other related inherited instincts mutated and transcended preprogrammed behaviour patterns because the phenomenon of memory and its associated learning functions broke the printed circuit. This led to altered behaviour patterns, while knowledge of past experience assisted man to develop his faculty of reason. Violence still exists; perhaps the new mammalian brain is still in an early stage of development or maybe the human life cycle actively lives out the various stages of its evolutionary development. Siff in contrast, asserts that man must be aware of the nature of his brain which constrains his natural impulses to the most primitive levels of behaviour. Altruistic behaviour, for example, cannot be attributed to an automatic consequence of evolution, but rather to the conscious use of the human mentation faculty to guide man in his actions.

The model of society postulated by Siff in this chapter is based on a hierarchy of five interlinked evolving concepts:

1. The *communal brain* which accounts for man's subconscious tendency to model his environment on the neurological systems of the human organism.
2. The *socio-brain* which defines any individual and technological system in a community which act like a group of cells.
3. The *socio-mind* which is the mentation faculty of the socio-brain of people who have similar thinking patterns, though they do not necessarily live in close geographical proximity to one another.
4. The *meta-socio-brain* comprises the global group of socio-brains and involves a clustering compulsion which results in the synthesis of individual brains into a global brain.
5. The *metasocio-mind* which describes the mentation faculty of the meta-socio-brain.

Although some of the concepts postulated by Melvyn Siff are fleetingly mentioned in a wide range of publications, most such references are poorly argued and no more than an eclectic synthesis of disparate ideas. While such writing may be of value in stimulating others in those research directions, it nevertheless remains for that group of researchers who are able to combine theory with practice to synthesize, develop and ultimately operationalize such concepts. This chapter is a pioneering work in this direction.

K.G.T.

A Bionic Model of Society*

The evolution of man has always been characterized by the persistent appearance of human agglomerations, known as communities. Since his earliest days, man, like the ants and the bees, has unconsciously succumbed to a compulsive centripetal force which has gathered him into relatively stable physical groups of various sizes and strengths.

This communal phenomenon attracted the attention of the father of cybernetic science, Norbert Wiener, who examined it in terms of homeostasis, or its error-correcting functioning. He observed that small communities generally exhibited considerable homeostasis, unlike their larger counterparts, about which he made the following remarks: "It is only in the large community, where the Lords of Things As They Are protect themselves from hunger by wealth, from public opinion by privacy and anonymity, from private criticism by the laws of libel and the possession of the means of communication, that ruthlessness can reach its most sublime levels. Of all these anti-homeostatic factors in society, the control of the means of communication is the most effective and the most important."[1]

This observation, based on Wiener's intimate knowledge of the science of control, is particularly relevant to a world which seems determined to descend into a bottomless pit of anti-homeostasis. The identification of communication as a major determinant of the stability of any community, particularly the world community, emerges as the most significant feature of the above assessment.

Therefore it becomes incumbent on the human race, especially those groups which wield the most power over the world's communication systems, to realize that the future of man depends on the efficient and ethical management of all communication systems, both human and technological.

Like the anthropologist who wonders at the complex phenomenon of man and attempts to retrace the elusive footprints of life, the cybernetician

---

* Each sub-section of this chapter has been summarized in the form of several observations to relieve the reader of the task of applying lengthy theory to the operational model of the final section.

cannot fail to reflect in his own terms on what led to the phenomenon of modern communication in all its varied forms.

The development of physical life-forms and the human consciousness which nurtured the abstractions of communication are inextricably linked. One cannot theorize about the two problems in isolation. The palaeontologist has to decipher the message of fossilized physical forms, while the researcher of communication has to decipher the abstract information which is fossilized in the form of words, language and minds.

The analysis must commence with an understanding of the human brain, which has always formed the nucleus of society and its communication networks.

The thinking brain seems to have sensed the limitations to its further evolution and has responded by devising ingenious technological prostheses to maintain its growth. Powered exo-skeletons in the form of modern vehicles have overcome many of the body's mechanical deficiencies, telecommunication devices have extended our short-ranged sensory and motor apparatus and medical science has supplemented the body's repair mechanisms. Photographic technology and sophisticated recording machines have extended the brain's memory system, while the electronic computer has expanded man's thinking ability.

As an inherent component of this global cybernetic organism, or "cyborg", we must examine not only the development of our society and its communication links, but also the purpose and limitations of human communications, and the future of society.

This study leads to the formulation of a model of society based on the working of the human brain and indicates how it may be used to guide the global communication process in a more synergistic direction.

Observation 1: Communication systems interfacing with the human brain are a major determinant of the stability of any community.
Observation 2: The future of man depends largely on the efficient and ethical management of all communication systems which interface with his brain.
Observation 3: The continuing evolution of the human mind is being facilitated by technological extensions of man's body and brain.

Models

Man has become an irrepressible architect of models, a designer of verbal and non-verbal representational forms. He uses models of all degrees of complexity to describe, predict or even control, phenomena and noumena.

He devises and manipulates models in situations where the size, complexity or accessibility of any system in his environment limits his ability to understand or manage the system itself. For instance, words, photographs, and mathematical equations all constitute models of systems in the "real world". One might suggest that the level of any person's mental sophistication may be judged by the degree of complexity of the models which he is able to create and usefully apply in his environment.

Models range in degree from the tangible to the intangible and may be classified into three general classes:[2]

The iconic model, which is a physical representation of the system being investigated. Such a model is directly descriptive of the real world and is typified by photographs or by the scale models of aircraft used in wind tunnels to study full-scale aircraft.

The analogue model, whose properties are similar to those of the actual system. For instance, the flow of water through pipes may sometimes be regarded as an analogue of the flow of electricity in conductors. The analogue computer can electronically simulate a host of real situations for rapid and convenient analysis.

The symbolic model, which is an abstract representation that uses symbols to describe certain features of a system. Mathematical models fall into this category.

Each class of model may be divided into one or more (further) categories – structural, functional or hybrid (structural-functional) – enabling us to construct a general classification table for models:

	STRUCTURAL	FUNCTIONAL
ICONIC	A	
ANALOGUE		B
SYMBOLIC		C

Figure 1: A classification scheme for models

For example, the position A would refer to a photograph of a system, B would refer to a water-flow analogue of an electric current and C to the mathematical form of Newton's second law of mechanics, $(F = \dfrac{d}{dt}(mv))$.

At best, any model can only offer a certain statistical probability of representing the activity of a complex system at any instant. Models of human groups are no exception, when one bears in mind that the behaviour of society depends on the largely unpredictable state of human consciousness. Since it is the aim of this chapter to construct a model of human society, the characteristics and limitations of the modelling process have to be considered from the start.

In designing a suitable model, it is important to anticipate whether the final product would be either too simplistic or too complex to be of significant value to the majority of social scientists. Just as a tin soldier model of interacting armies would be of highly limited use to most scientists, so would a highly abstract mathematical description of human behaviour be of little immediate significance to the average non-mathematically minded social scientists. For this reason, a hybrid analogue has been selected to satisfy a wider audience. The interested reader should then be able to modify the model in either an iconic or a symbolic direction to suit his particular needs.

No modeller of society can afford to ignore the fact that collective human behaviour is just as much a function of the human body and brain as is the behaviour of the individual. The brain, in particular, may be regarded as the seat of human government. This selfsame view was expressed in the fifth century B.C. by the father of medical science, Hippocrates, who said:
"From the brain and the brain alone, arise our pleasures, joys, . . . as well as our sorrows, pain, grief and tears. Through it, in particular, we think, see, hear and distinguish the ugly from the beautiful, the bad from the good . . . It is the same thing which makes us mad or delirious, inspires us with dread or fear, whether by night or by day. It brings sleeplessness, inopportune mistakes, aimless anxieties, absent-mindedness, and acts that are contrary to habit."[3]

Having identified the brain as the fundamental determinant of human group behaviour, it now becomes necessary to complete the inventory of other important features which have to be taken account of in synthesizing a model of society. These are as follows:
- the central nervous system, including the brain, and its relevance to consciousness and behaviour;
- the nature of the sensory inputs and motor outputs which enable man to interact with others and his environment;
- the formation, growth and decay of human groups;
- the communication systems which integrate the individual into society and the environment;
- the technological advances which have facilitated contact between distant groups;

- the phenomenon of leadership and government;
- the existence of religious and ethical codes to control individuals and groups;
- the preservation of identity by individuals in groups or by groups within groups;
- the vastly differing degrees of scientific and cultural advancement among human groups;
- the use of communication systems to programme and control groups;
- the role of the environment;
- the phenomenon of mind;
- the persistence of isolated groups;
- the broad spectrum of groups ranging in nature from the physical to the mental.

The above features will now be examined to ascertain whether they can be integrated into a single comprehensive model of society.

At no stage should there be recourse to the Procrustean method, in which reality is distorted to fit the model. Procrustes, of course, was the fabulous Greek robber who cut his guests to the correct size for their beds.

Observation 4: It is necessary for man to devise models or representations of "reality" in situations where the size, complexity or accessibility of any system limits his ability to understand or manage the system itself.

Observation 5: The brain may be regarded as the seat of human government.

Observation 6: Any acceptable model of society must account for the important characteristics of the individual and the group. In particular, special prominence should be given to the role of man's brain-mind complex and his communication systems.

Preliminary considerations

There are certain inherent problems of human communication which concern our sensory organs, our language systems and basic philosophical issues.

It is well known that man's sensory inputs admit only a very narrow spectrum of information. In addition, the highly filtered data flow is processed all along the neural pathways even before the brain constructs a model of what the senses have perceived. The identification of and response to the mental model depends on the previous experience, or memory codes, programmed into the brain during earlier encounters with society. For these reasons alone, metaphysical reality can be seen as meaningless when viewed in the context of the central nervous system. In all transactions with the environment the brain employs a language of abstract neural modelling and it is natural that human language, as a product of the human brain, must involve even more approximate modelling of "reality".

Benjamin Lee Whorf remarked that "language is an organ of the mind" and acts like the sensory organs in filtering and distorting environmental data. A theory relevant to this assessment, has been propounded by H. Jerrison considering language as a by-product of its basic role in the construction of reality. According to his theory, language, a non-physical organ of the developing mind, evolved as a further aid to providing an adequate model to the sensory events experienced by man. He stated: "We need language more to tell stories than to direct actions. In the telling we create mental images in our listeners that might normally be produced only by the memory of events as recorded and integrated by the sensory and perceptual systems of the brain."[4]

In the light of such knowledge about our sensory receptors and language systems, we might summarize the position in the form of a

Communications Uncertainty Principle:

> The observer and the observed interact with one another in such a way that the state of the observed may not be defined precisely at any instant in any language by the observer.

Not only do our senses admit the passage of highly selected information to the brain, but they are unable to respond to most of the information arising from our environment. Our eyes limit our sight to the narrow visible spectrum of electro-magnetic radiation, while our ears limit our hearing to sound waves which vibrate at a frequency of between 20 and 20 000 cycles per second. Our bodies are unable to sense radio waves, cosmic radiation, ultrasonic sound waves, X-rays and magnetic fields. Our coarse sense of vision does not permit us to see cells, molecules, atoms, electrons and other microscopic particles. If it did, we would experience the apparent solidity of our environment as a vast expanse of space interrupted by whirling vortices of scintillating energy-matter. Our experience of the universe indeed is determined by the constraints imposed by our sensory systems and brains.

Scientific instruments have extended our senses into the macroscopic and microscopic universe, yet our experience of the universe remains far from ambiguous.

Perhaps we will always remain in the same position as hypothetical two-dimensional bugs whose eyes limit them to seeing events in a flat plane. Should a three-dimensional spherical ball bounce into the world, they will see only a succession of appearing and disappearing circular discs. (Figure 2)

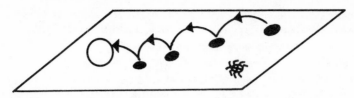

Figure 2: The world of a two-dimensional bug

Their experience of a sphere thus will be restricted to the region of contact between the sphere and their world. Should one bug ascend a hump rising from his world, while his companion remains on a planar region, they will suddenly become invisible to one another (Fig. 3).

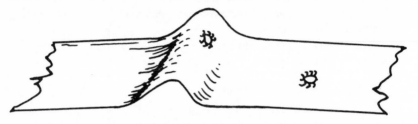

Figure 3: One case of invisibility in two dimensions

Such a world may appear to be fantastic, but it is not dissimilar to our universe in which sub-atomic particles appear and disappear, particles act like waves, and mass increases with velocity. Just as two-dimensional bugs are limited to a two-dimensional experience of their universe, so we are physically limited to a three-dimensional experience of our environment. Our very nature precludes us from directly experiencing anything which extends into multi-dimensional space. We can only theorize about those things which elude our senses.

The uncertainty of any communication is compounded further by our narrow experience of objects and events in space and time. Modern science has uncovered an unsuspected universe which seems to violate all "common sense". Space and time can no longer be regarded as separate entities, nor can matter be separated from energy. A single "particle" like an electron can pass through several coplanar holes simultaneously, so that particles sometimes behave more like waves. Einstein's theory of relativity reveals that we have to abandon the Newtonian concepts of absolute space and time, since mass, length and time vary with the motion of the observer. Gravitation affects the passage of both light and time, and force may be envisaged as the interchange of certain invisible particles. Space, time, matter and a host of other basic concepts of our environment now have to be seen as convenient language symbols which we use to describe certain phenomena. "Reality" seems to be more unattainable to man than it ever has been, so it is not unexpected to find humans disagreeing violently on the basis of their distorted images of the same event.

The concept of a linear, sequential time flow is by no means universal or obvious. As Einstein stated: "The separation between past, present and future has only the meaning of an illusion, albeit a tenacious one." [5]

The language of the Trobriand Islanders and the Hopi Indians of America reveals that they have a viewpoint which is similar to Einstein's. [6] In the case of the Hopi Indians, who have no concept of past, present and future, they have terms which can be translated roughly as objective (manifest) or subjective (unmanifest). The "objective" embraces all objects and events that are or have been accessible to the senses, which therefore includes past and present. The "subjective" refers to all events that appear in the mind, of which the future is only a part. [7] Moreover, the Hopis believe that each creature possesses its own reference system and events experienced by a specific creature occur relative to that creature's reference system. Experience of any event therefore is relative to the consciousness of the observing creature, a concept which is closely analogous to Einstein's relativity theory.

Despite the existence of relatively stable bioelectrical and biochemical rhythms in the body, man possesses no sensory mode which is able to respond directly to "time". There is a distinct difference between "clock time" and "psychological time".

A person's experience of time depends on his psychological or physiological state and, in particular, seems to bear some relationship to his level of emotional arousal, the frequency of his brain rhythms and his body temperature. The language of mathematics permits us to take account of subjectivity, or relativity, in physical systems, but daily language as yet contains no term which enables us to describe subjective, or psychological, time. Time continues to be regarded as an infinite linear space which may be divided into sequences of smaller segments. Absolute "clock time" moulds our awareness of that which is referred to as "time" and the underlying "reality" remains buried under the debris of inadequate terminology.

All the constraints which are imposed by our bodies may be stated in the form of a *Communications Relativity Principle:*

> Experience of any event is relative to the state of activation of the sensory and neural apparatus of the observer at the instant of observation.

Philosophical issues

Besides the problems concerning language and man's sensory apparatus, two philosophical issues raised by Kurt Gödel place further obstacles in the path of a straight-forward assessment of communication. The first issue concerns change. Up to this point, the term "evolution" has been used loosely in its popular context. However, Gödel refuses to accept the objectivity of change and considers it to be yet another illusion caused by our special mode of perception.[8] Since change is related to our concept of linear time, one's initial impulse to dismiss Gödel's conclusion has to be held in check.

Gödel's second issue is his better-known meta-mathematical Incompleteness Theorem of 1931: "No calculus can be devised in such a way that every arithmetical proposition is represented in it by a formula which is either 'provable' or 'disprovable' within the calculus,"[9] i.e. even in elementary arithmetic there exist propositions which cannot be proved in that system. Although this theorem seems to be purely mathematical in nature, its wider implication is that the mind cannot prove formally the consistency of a system by using the system itself. It appears as if man's understanding of himself and the universe is destined to rely heavily on the scientifically indefinable process of intuition.

Those who question the application of Gödel's theorem to human systems should bear in mind that a similar conclusion may be reached from a consideration of the Second Law of Thermodynamics, as applied to communication. Since the entropy, or "degree of disorder" of any closed system, tends to increase with time, no information can be transmitted with perfect fidelity within a system. Every transmitted message experiences some distortion, and the intelligibility of any information depends on its signal-to-noise ratio. If the signal strength diminishes or the noise level rises sufficiently, the message might become totally unintelligible, as in the case of a distant, indistinct telephone call. In other words, it is a law of nature that all communication must become distorted to a greater or lesser degree. Since some form of communication is necessary for observation of all phenomena in the universe, this inherent noisiness of information transmission constrains man to an imprecise view of everything that constitutes his world.

Observation 7: The human senses are highly selective filters which restrict man's view of the environment to a narrow spectrum of information.

Observation 8: Language behaves like an organ of the mind to restrict man's experience of the universe to approximate models of "reality".

Observation 9: Modern science reveals that the most basic physical concepts such as matter, space and time are not objective phenomena, but are language symbols whose meaning is relative to the observer's mental programmes.

Observation 10: It is an implication of Gödel's theorem and the Second Law of Thermodynamics that man is constrained to an inprecise view of his environment.

The clustering compulsion

It has always been necessary for the individual to live in symbiotic or parasitic relationships with other people. Without this group compulsion, families, tribes and nations would not have emerged. Armies, educational institutions, governments and all the organizations which typify modern society would not exist to-day, nor would there be any point in my writing these words or any words at all, for there would be no reason for communicating this information to that type of fellow man who wishes to remain a compulsive hermit.

The following question immediately arises: Why do individuals cluster into groups? At this point, it suffices to suggest that consideration of Maslow's hierarchy of needs supplies a plausible answer, namely that man is gregarious because it satisfies one or more of his fundamental needs:

- physiological
- safety
- belongingness and love
- self-esteem
- self-actualization

At a later stage in this chapter this answer will be adapted to incorporate the experimental evidence of current neuropsychological research into human behaviour.

The clustering tendency of man has facilitated the evolution of the individual mind and the collective mind, mediated largely by the development of extensive communication linkages. Modern man no longer interfaces with his fellow man alone, but he also interfaces with a host of technological systems varying from microscopes to spacecraft and computers. The schoolboy of to-day is no longer ''a noise surrounded by dirt'' but an evolving being interfacing with technological prostheses such as electronic pocket-calculators.

In fact, the clustering compulsion may be regarded as a specific instance of what may be termed the human interfacing drive, man's propensity for interfacing with a large variety of animate and inanimate systems in his environment. The human-centred interfacing system may be represented diagrammatically as follows:

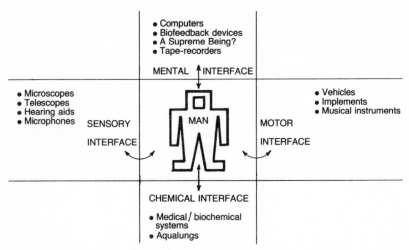

Figure 4: The human-centred interfacing system. (The arrows represent communication links across interfaces.)

For example, at the motor interface, man interfaces with vehicles and the machinery of war; at the sensory interface he extends his senses by means of microscopes and telescopes, and at the mental interface, he supplements his neural capabilities by the use of computers and tape-recorders.

It should be remembered that man frequently communicates across several interfaces at once and that the interfaces are not necessarily discrete. In interfacing with other people, we usually communicate across several interfaces to form that complex human-interfacing system known as society.

No other organism displays a compulsion and ingenuity comparable to man's for interfacing with systems of nature or of his own creation. This fact is a more compelling demonstration of man's mental uniqueness than the more esoteric arguments based on comparisons between the minds of man and animals.

In effect, this means that any model of society must account for man as a multi-faceted interfacing system in both the individual and the communal setting. This necessitates an understanding of the neuropsychological-biochemical basis of human behaviour and the significance of the communication matrix which facilitates group coherence.

Observation 11: Man forms groups to satisfy one or more of his basic needs as classified by Maslow.

Observation 12: Man is characterized by an interfacing drive which compels him to establish communication links across sensory, motor, chemical and mental interfaces in his environment. Interpersonal interfacing is a particular case of this phenomenon.

Observation 13: Man's uniqueness is emphasized by his compulsion and ingenuity for interfacing with systems of nature or of his own creation.

Human drive

Accepting that man's gregariousness may be explained in terms of Maslow's hierarchy of needs, we still have to answer the question: why does man need? – what causes his drives? Even if man has been defined as possessing a powerful "human interfacing drive", why does he want to interface and form communities?

An answer seems to be emerging from the experiments involving electrical stimulation of the brain.

About 20 years ago, the psychologist James Old, who was investigating the effects of electrical excitation on the brains of live rats, discovered that the animals would deliberately close switches for the sole purpose of experiencing a tiny electric shock via electrodes implanted in the limbic system. The rats sought no other reward than electrical activation of certain regions in this "primitive" part of the brain. Years of experimentation with animals and humans have established that electrical stimulation of these areas elicits distinct pleasure, sometimes of such intensity that animals will ignore all other rewards such as food and sex to depress incessantly the switch which provides the electrical activation. To reach the "pleasure switch", rats will negotiate highly uncomfortable obstacles which provide vigorous electric shocks. For obvious reasons, these regions have come to be known as the "pleasure" or "reward" centres of the brain.

Other experiments have revealed the existence of other centres in the brain which animals strenuously avoid stimulating. Excitation of these "displeasure" or "punishment" centres can cause a variety of reactions including terror, rage, aggression, flight and pain.

These discoveries have prompted Professor John Taylor to remark: "It would seem from these findings that heaven and hell have been located inside the human brain. They are not in the sky above or deep in the bowels of the earth, but in our own brains." [10]

Pleasure or displeasure centres should not be regarded as simple homogeneous groups of neurons whose specific purpose is mediation of pleasant or unpleasant responses. They are complex multi-purpose regions of brain tissue whose functioning is dependent on an intricate sequence of biochemical and bioelectric events.

The degree of pleasure experienced is a function of the intensity of the stimulating current and there is an optimum strength which excites man or beast to depress the "pleasure switch" at the greatest rate. As the current strength is decreased below this optimum value, the pressing frequency decreases and ultimately stops. A similar response follows an increase of current above this optimum value, and in addition, the animal deliberately avoids touching the switch again. A probable explanation is that high intensity electrical activity tends to spread to nearby punishment centres, which are usually found a matter of a few millimetres distant from the pleasure centres.

Activation of territory between pleasure and punishment centres causes ambivalent response in an animal. The creature vacillates between an ardent pressing of the switch and a determined avoidance of it. This phenomenon, labelled variously as the "stop it, I like it" reaction or the "go on, you're hurting me" response, may account for masochistic and sadistic behaviour. [11]

Pleasure elicited by ordinary sensory stimulation also serves as a highly-prized reward for living creatures, but the normal brain seems to possess a governing device which prevents incessant peripheral self-stimulation. Nevertheless, the existence of sensory pathways to the limbic system apparently ensures that man's behaviour is dependent on stimulation of his "pleasure" and "punishment" centres. The theological concept of a heavenly final state appears to be an intuitive statement of man's basic neural programme to seek pleasure and diminish pain.

The subconscious persistence of pleasure might even be the prime motive behind an animal's will to live. The centres which control life's vital functions such as respiration, olfaction, feeding, biological rhythms, sexual behaviour and emotion are in close proximity to the pleasure centres, so it may not be unreasonable to speculate that the activity associated with the vital processes could cause an unspecific intrinsic pleasure of which all creatures are subconsciously aware.

Decreased activation of the pleasure centres or increased activation of the punishment centres causes "need", which may be defined as a type of neural pain. Maslow's hierarchy of needs, therefore, may be considered as a hierarchy of different patterns of neural "pain" associated with the activation of progressively more extensive regions of the brain. At the lowest and most essential physiological level, the "primitive" regions of the brain would be the major determinant of need, while at the highest self-actualizing level, most of the brain would define the need.

It is interesting to follow this process from its source, the evolving human mind.

The newborn infant enters the world with a largely undeveloped brain and certain autonomic and instinctive functions which offer a basis for his survival. If one looks quite dispassionately at modern scientific evidence, one tends to agree strongly with Professor Delgado's conclusion that the human being is born without a mind. [12] The development of mind is not automatic, but depends on the existence of determined programmers such as parents and teachers who utilize the child's sensory inputs to enable the brain to structure a mind.

The child has to reach adulthood before it becomes capable of self-programming, but until then it remains a programmable machine whose ontogenesis is determined by the external manipulation of its pleasure and punishment centres.

The child grows up and later programmes its own offspring; the programmed becomes the programmer and further intelligent units join the vast collection of human cells which constitute the collective brain. The clustering compulsion of man, determined somehow by years of patterned activation of certain neural zones within each person, becomes assured of a future, and the phenomenon of society persists as a characteristic of mankind.

The cycle continues, guaranteeing the presence of other beings to enhance the possibility of stimulation for the pleasure areas of our brains. The collective brain stimulates the individual brain and vice versa. Too much or too little stimulation leads to diminished coherence of the communal brain.

Future research may well cause a drastic revision or abandonment of the pleasure (or anti-pain) theory of behaviour. Nevertheless there is little doubt that human behaviour ultimately will be explained in terms of highly complex physical and chemical events in the brain. At the present stage of knowledge of the brain it probably would be more accurate to talk generally about behaviour being determined by programmed patterns or rhythms of bioelectrical or biochemical activity in the central nervous system.

We cannot escape the obvious implication that most of man's behaviour, concepts and beliefs are associated with electrical activity within the limbic system, the deep-seated subhuman core of the brain. Much of our attitude towards ourselves and other people is therefore a consequence of primitive emotional involvement caused by years of sensory-motor stimulation of the brain.

It is upon this foundation that human communication and social behaviour is based.

Observation 14: Man's emotional response to information reaching his brain via the senses is related to stimulation of pleasure (reward) or pain (punishment) centres in a primitive region of the brain known as the limbic system.
Observation 15: The development of the human mind is not automatic but is achieved by external programming of the growing child's brain by parents and other educators.
Observation 16: Most of man's behaviour, concepts and beliefs are associated with electrical activation of the limbic system.

The communal brain

Somatic modelling

Most of us are familiar with Jung's psychological theory of archetypal symbols which form part of man's fundamental inner language system.[13] Certain recurring symbols appearing in words, dreams and art seem to be common to all mankind and most of our externalized language apparently is based on this subconscious encyclopaedia of inherent mental hieroglyphs. It is not surprising that many of these thought-forms involve parts of the body, the object with which each person is most closely involved.

In his study of the origin and symbolism of human language, Thass-Thienemann reached the following conclusion:
"All vocal language, in a general sense, is somatic expression. The psychosomatic identity of body and mind is still rooted in the biological needs and their subjective perception, out of which all higher, and more abstract, forms of symbolization developed . . . The body symbolism of the vocal language cannot be deciphered any more, in most cases, because its origins lie in the prehistoric past. It appears in our mental apparatus, as unconscious, and for this reason it is open to analytical interpretation . . . man perceives, thinks, and speaks in terms of his own body and bodily functions."[14]

Such a conclusion is not surprising when one considers the preoccupation of generations of developing children with the body and its functions. Not only are the first few years of an infant's life spent in intensive somatic exploration, but the onset of puberty also arouses in the adolescent a vigorous awareness of the body.

Recent neuropsychological findings offer corroborative evidence for the occurrence of innate mental symbols. It has been known for centuries that migraine,[15] pressure on the eye-balls, and blows on the head ("seeing stars") can cause vivid visual displays even in a person whose eyes are closed. These patterns, known as phosphenes, also may be evoked by electrical or magnetic stimulation of the optic pathways or other parts of the brain. Furthermore, even in the dark, retinal ganglion cells produce fairly regular impulses at a frequency of 20 to 30 cycles per second.

Researchers such as Oster have noted the intensity similarity between the most common phosphenes and the basic geometric shapes of both primitive and modern art, thereby offering a physiological basis for archetypal images.[16]

Other experiments have revealed that parts of the brain associated with vision are arranged in regular columns of nervous tissue.[17] This structural and functional organization implies that visual perception of our environment involves processing of input information in straight parallel lines, so that planar straight-line geometry seems to be eminently compatible with our neural apparatus.[15, 17, 18] In the words of Stent, ". . . neurobiology has now shown why it is human to hold Euclidean geometry and its non-intersecting coplanar parallel lines to be a self-evident truth. Non-Euclidean geometrics of convex or concave surfaces, although our brain is evidently capable of conceiving them, are more alien to our built-in spatial-perception processes."[19]

Such evidence not only emphasizes that the nature of the brain places definite constraints on man's transactions with himself and others, but it also leads me to suggest that *the brain acts as a structural and functional archetype for the social group.*

Man subconsciously seems to model his environment on the systems of the body, hence society may well have evolved as an externalized model of the brain. Indeed, the human community, like the brain, comprises a complex system of cells interacting by means of a communication network which transports material and information. One wonders whether man will continue to project his inner space and its workings onto his outer space and use regular feedback to modify his model until one day there will be little functional distinction between man's inner and outer worlds.

In other words, the clustering compulsion seems to be evidence of a subconscious human drive to synthesize individual brains into a global brain in pursuit of nature's evolutionary trend from simple unicellular to complex multicellular existence.

Despite human behaviour to the contrary, the obvious climax of this process is a synergistic global organism in which the component brains retain their individuality yet co-operate via an extensive communication network to produce a total capability which surpasses the sum of the capabilities of all the separate brains.

Even if the social group is not considered as a projected archetype of the brain, the human brain may be used as a valuable analogue of the human community. As a highly successful composite of millions of discrete active units, the brain may be regarded as a particularly suitable model of that other complex matrix of millions of vital units, the global social group.

Such a model may be termed "bionic", if we consider Steele's original definition of bionics as "the science of systems whose function is based on living systems or which have characteristics of living systems, or which resemble these".[20] If we refer to Gérardin's modified definition: "Bionics is the art of applying the knowledge of living systems to solving technical problems",[21] we can infer that a bionic model of society should offer a means of managing the social problems of mankind.

It remains the final task of this chapter to develop this bionic "neural model" of society further and use it to suggest possible ways of solving the major problems of society.

Observation 17: The instinctive preoccupation of man with his body and its functions lays the foundations for every person's perception and description of himself, others and his environment.

Observation 18: Man's percepts and concepts are shaped by the structural and functional organization of his brain.

Observation 19: The human brain acts as a structural and functional archetype for the social group.

Observation 20: Man's clustering compulsion suggests a subconscious drive to synthesize individual brains into a global brain to continue the evolutionary trend from unicellularity to multicellularity.

Observation 21: The human brain may be used as a suitable bionic model of the social group.

The socio-brain and socio-mind

Any individuals living together act like a group of cells in what may be termed a socio-brain, the latter including any technological devices such as computers which contribute to its existence and evolution. All the communication systems within such a socio-brain behave like the network of nerves within the human brain and permit interfacing between individuals in the group. It is clear that the coherence of the group depends on the nature of the communication network and its use by influential members as a means of controlling the group.

The socio-brain of the group, in turn, has associated with it a socio-mind determined by the collected minds of all the people in the group.

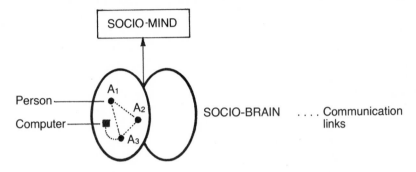

Figure 5: Composition of the basic group socio-brain

The entire human society consists of numerous such groups ranging in size from families and tribes to cities and nations, living together in geographic, though not necessarily mental, proximity. Modern communication has enabled many of these groups to interface with one another so that individuals who have more in common with colleagues outside their own geographic or physical group coalesce mentally to form their specific socio-brain.

This model is expressed most effectively in the form of a diagram which shows how different groups contribute to the formation of a metasocio-brain with its own metasocio-mind comprising the socio-mind of each group, together with the socio-minds of physically separate, though mentally attached, individuals (see Fig. 6).

In the diagram on p. 98, we can see that socio-brain A comprising the individual people A_1, A_2, and A_3 has a socio-mind A associated with it. Similarly, socio-brain C has its own socio-mind C. In addition, individuals A_2 and C_2 in the two different groups are mentally linked via the communication system which connects the socio-brains A and C, resulting in their common socio-mind AC. Since individuals in socio-brains A and C are associated with the socio-minds A and C as well as the socio-mind AC, there will be an intersection of both socio-mind A and socio-mind C with socio-mind AC (the shaded regions).

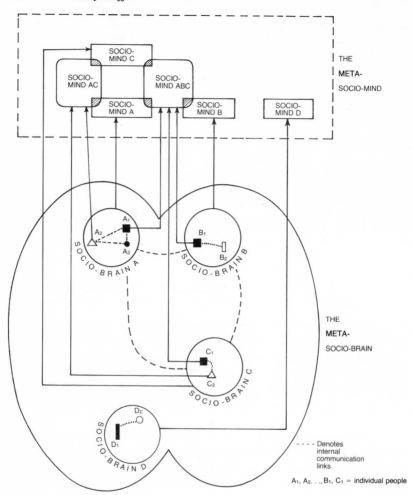

Figure 6: The metasocio-brain and metasocio-mind

Socio-brain D refers, for example, to an isolated primitive group with no communication link to the outside world. Obviously, such a society can have little influence on the metasocio-mind of the combined socio-minds until part of the global communication network reaches out to embrace this waif of mental evolution. The term metasocio-mind may be applied to the communal mind of any large group of people, be it a city, nation or the world community.

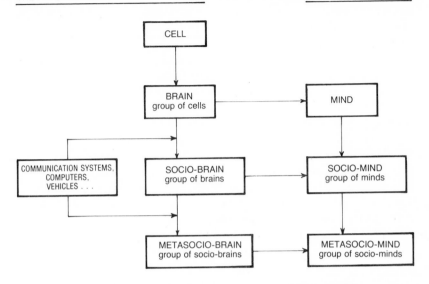

Figure 7: Relationship between concepts used in the model

In this model the term "socio-brain" is associated with physical grouping whereas the term "socio-mind" is associatd with grouping of minds, even if the people involved are physically separated. However, the existence of any meaningful socio-mind depends on definite communication channels linking the separate minds. It is unrealistic to postulate the existence of some esoteric system which facilitates the sort of mental coalescence envisaged by Teilhard de Chardin for millions of individuals who may not be linked by any physical communication system. For those who might be interested in extending this model into the realm of mysticism, they could consider the development of the human mind as a precursor to a possible coalescence of sets of metasocio-minds into a "meta-metasocio-mind"!

For those who wish to keep their feet on the ground, let them consider the growth of the social group as analogous to the growth of the human brain from the moment of conception within the womb.

The pattern of human growth from conception to adulthood is considered by some to parallel the evolution of man from the earliest life-form. Man's development from a fertilized cell to the thinking adult is viewed as a time-compressed version of man's evolution over eons of history. What required millions of years now takes place in less than two decades. The human rises through the stages of being an aquatic foetus, a relatively mindless beast crawling on all fours, a primate able to manipulate artefacts and finally, homo sapiens at the pinnacle of evolution. Whether such an hypothesis is valid or not is unimportant: this concept still provides a useful description of the evolution of the socio-mind.

The socio-brain develops like the child's brain. The number of brain cells increases in distinct phases of growth and after the birth of a child or a group, the environment provides a medium for increasing the richness of interconnections in the brain or socio-brain. A stimulating environment which provides abundant physical and mental nutriment results in a person or community of superior ability. But, just as a highly intelligent person can become a criminal, so can a highly developed community display aberrant behaviour: witness, for instance, the recent Nazi horror. A highly developed socio-mind has become a characteristic of modern society, but a synergistic socio-mind has so far eluded the efforts of religions, governments, the League of Nations and the United Nations. Clearly, a scientifically and religiously sophisticated socio-mind is no guarantee of utopia.

The programme for the physical nature and development of the human brain is transmitted from parent to child, from generation to generation, by means of biochemical entities known as genes. Similarly the programme for the nature and development of the socio-brain may be attributed indirectly to the human genes. At the level of the socio-mind, the persistence of the clustering compulsion and social ideas may be considered to be a consequence of programmes transmitted in the form of mind-genes or noogenes.

Jacques Monod, joint recipient of the 1965 Nobel prize for his contribution to deciphering the genetic code, laid the foundation for the concept of a noogene by discussing the "performance value" or "promotion value" of an idea in the following terms: "The performance value of an idea depends on the change it brings to the behaviour of the person or the group that adopts it. The human group upon which a given idea confers greater cohesiveness, greater ambition, and greater self-confidence thereby receives from it an added power to expand which will insure the promotion of the idea itself. Its promotion value bears no relation to the amount of objective truth the idea may contain . . . The spreading power of an idea . . . depends upon pre-existing structures in the mind, among them ideas already implanted by culture, but undoudtedly upon certain innate structures which are very difficult for us to identify." [22]

In other words, the characteristics of society such as government, religion, educational systems, ideologies and language, like the structure of the human body, seem to be determined by special types of gene.

The evolution of these non-physical noogenes has been facilitated by the clustering compulsion of man, which has resulted in the creation of vast communication systems to transmit each noogene as it develops. The existence of sizeable communities has provided a testing ground for ideas which have been disseminated via the communication network within each group. It is interesting to note that Hall goes as far as saying that mind is really internalized culture.[23]

As discussed earlier, the instinctive preoccupation of man with his body and its functions lays the foundation for every person's perception and description of himself, others and his environment. The noogenes develop within groups of human minds and are constrained to a limited variety of patterns by man's subconscious propensity for thinking in terms of somatic symbolism.

A similar concept of social genes has been considered for somewhat different reasons by Dawkins who proposes the "meme" as the unit of imitation or cultural transmission.[24] He suggests that the meme is a cultural replicator of such evolutionary import that it is far outstripping the physical gene in significance.

In an appraisal of this hypothesis, Humphrey states that ". . . memes should be regarded as living structures, not just metaphorically but technically. When you plant a fertile meme in my mind you literally parasitise my brain, turning it into a vehicle for the meme's propagation in just the way that a virus may parasitise the genetic mechanism of a host cell. And this isn't just a way of talking – the meme for, say, 'belief in life after death' is actually realised physically, millions of times over, as a structure in the nervous systems of individual men the world over." [25]

The existence of influential ideas-men and communication systems emerges as vital to the development and proliferation of noogenes and the behaviour of the society which they determine.

The acceptance of particular noogenes as programmes for the evolution of society depends on their appeal to the socio-mind of any group. In the individual brain, acceptance of a concept is associated with the pleasure or preferred neural patterns elicited by processing of the message. Widespread adoption of an idea by a group of people may be attributed to the mass effect of stimulation of the "pleasure" or "reward" areas of the group's socio-brain. Conditioning of individuals and groups thus may be seen to be mediated through the primitive or limbic region of the brain.

Acceptance of unpleasant ideas by members within a group may in some respects be regarded as mental masochism.

It is important to recognize that each socio-mind is a dynamic system displaying different degrees of consciousness determined by the state of activation of the socio-brain associated with it. Just as the individual brain experiences phases of sleep and wakefulness, so the socio-brain experiences its own phases of consciousness. This is due to the fact that at any particular moment every person within a group exhibits a different state of consciousness and emotion, related to whatever system or other person he is interfacing with at that instant.

The state of consciousness of a person is reflected by the electrical rhythms produced by his brain, specific patterns and frequencies being associated with different mental states and different regions of the brain. The origin of the electroencephalogram apparently lies in the spontaneous activity of millions of nerve cells co-ordinated rhythmically by groups of pacemaking nuclei within the thalamus[26]. Similarly, influential persons or groups act as foci for controlling large communities within the metasocio-brain, the extent of their control being determined by the effectiveness of the communication systems involved. However, unlike the thalamic nuclei of the normal brain, the most powerful human foci within the metasocio-mind rarely act automatically in a synergistic fashion. The rise of dangerous leaders to power is equivalent to anti-homeostatic forces appearing in certain regions of the brain as tumours, cancers or other diseases of the neural tissue. The result may be paroxysmal convulsion, insanity, paralysis, coma or even death of the afflicted socio-brain. The group may disintegrate, atrophy, radiate in a destructive path through other groups or recoil on its leaders or foci. History has been punctuated with monotonous regularity by the emergence and evanescence of such foci within the metasocio-brain.

The effect of drugs such as alcohol, marijuana, the alkaloids, LSD and the barbiturates is due to their modification of the bioelectrical and biochemical activity existing in the communication pathways of the brain. An analogous manipulation of the socio-brain is achieved by government control of the communication systems within any nation. Propaganda, like a behaviour-modifying drug, is infused into the communication stream of the socio-brain and the opportunity for individual mental inoculation against the intruder is minimized because all governments have extensive control over the mass media. Just as physical and mental nutriment play a decisive role in the development of the human brain, so doctrinal nutriment fed by educational institutions to the socio-brain plays a vital role in the evolution of society. Governments or rulers thereby strive to prevent the mutation of noogenes into a template for behaviour which does not conform to their packaged programmes. The lesson of history is clear in this regard: evolution is a patient process and has time on its side in the inexorable pursuit of its goal.

Society might take heed of what happens to a person who is deprived of varied sensory stimulation. The experiments of researchers such as Lilly revealed that sensory deprivation can lead to hallucinations and "disorganization of brain function similar to, and in some respects as great as, that produced by drugs or lesions".[27] We can infer that any socio-brain which is not exposed to regular stimulation of sufficient variety is liable to manifest aberrant behaviour. Imaginings may become reality and a social psychosis is likely to undermine the integrity of that socio-brain.

Another important observation is that each socio-brain is characterized by a different starting point, rate of evolution, size, technology, physical resources and racial composition. Socio-brains appear, amalgamate or disappear and it will be a long time before every community becomes a meaningful component of the ideal homeostatic metasocio-mind served by an all-embracing communication network. In this respect, the human brain far surpasses the metasocio-brain in excellence of structure and function.

It would be interesting to continue this analogy between the brain and the social group, for there are numerous relevant neural functions which parallel the behaviour of society. For instance, the left hemisphere of the brain is associated with logical thought processes, while the right hemisphere concerns intuitive and artistic processes. Eastern culture relies heavily on intuitive thought, whereas Western culture is highly scientific and logical in nature. Therefore, Eastern and Western groups might be regarded as components of the right and left hemispheres of the metasocio-brain, respectively.

Sufficient background information has been provided to show that the social group not only acts like a brain, but that it is an evolving brain of growing complexity.

It now remains to apply this socio-brain model in a brief analysis of some problems of society.

Observation 22: Any individuals and technological systems in a community act like a group of cells in constituting a "socio-brain". On a global level, there is a "metasocio-brain" comprising groups of socio-brains.

Observation 23: The mentation facility of the socio-brain or metasocio-brain may be described in terms of the socio-mind or metasocio-mind respectively.

Observation 24: The socio-brain develops from conception to death like the human brain in structure and function.

Observation 25: The existence of mind-genes, or "noogenes", ensures the transmission of cultural concepts from generation to generation.

Observation 26: Propaganda and similar mental programmes infused via communication systems into the communal mind elicit different states of consciousness in the socio-brain just as behaviour-modifying drugs do in the individual brain.

Observation 27: Influential individuals in the socio-brain behave like vital foci in the brain in co-ordinating the activity of groups of cells.

Towards a solution

Man cannot forever remain a passive spectator at the living exhibition of antihomeostasis that is modern society. It is an abrogation of our duties to bequeath the problems of society to a delitescent Supreme Being. Sufficient numbers of mentally evolved individuals have emerged to recognize that the solution lies in their actively becoming foci from which a universal code of human cybernetic principles or noo-ecology can radiate.

Cybernetics has provided the necessary theoretical background, but intellectual pleasure-seeking must be accompanied by practical and ethical applications of the abstract principles. For instance, the abstract concepts of

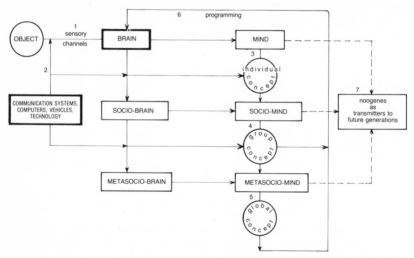

Figure 8: The operation of the socio-model. The boxes in bold outline indicate the key elements of the model

this chapter may be put to more useful account if summarized in the form of a diagram (Figure 8) upon which we can focus our attention in formulating solutions to the problems inherent in social grouping.

The model operates in the following way. An object or event is conveyed to the brain via the sensory channels, 1, possibly augmented by various communication or other technological systems, 2. The mind produces its particular individual concept, 3, of this object or event, which is transmitted to the socio-mind. The latter draws from the concept pool of its component minds, and a series of widely accepted group concepts, 4, emerge. At the highest level, the processing of group concepts within the metasocio-mind produces global concepts, 5, which are generally acceptable to all mankind.

The group and global concepts are fed back to the individual brain by educators and governments as socially desirable programmes, 6, and act as major determinants of individual and group behaviour. These programmes, as well as the structure and function of the brain, prescribe how man responds to the information perceived through his senses. The entire process ensures that a library of noogenetic information, 7, is created and sustained for transmission to future generations.

Indisputably, the foundations of a stable noo-ecology lie in the human brain and the use of the technological extensions of our bodies, in particular the mass communication systems. Therefore any realistic solutions should take account of the design, operation and control of these components of the metasocio-brain, or global community.

Religion, as the universal panacea, has offered packaged sets of rules to guide man in a direction of greater harmony, or homeostasis, but has failed to provide man with the theoretical background which is necessary for the destruction of the cancer of superstition within itself.

Religions have not evolved sufficiently to absorb the discoveries of the scientific revolution into their philosophies. Man is no longer satisfied with dogma: he demands rational explanations and scientific proofs. Religion has responded by outlawing science as a bumptious atheistic usurper of divine authority, instead of recognizing that science is merely striving to mutate religion into a less anachronistic philosophy. Religion now has the choice of accepting mutation of its noogenetic information or of losing influence to the flood of scientific noogenes.

In contrasting the behaviour of social insects (ants, bees, termites) with that of man, Monod states the following:

"The invention of myths and religions, the construction of vast philosophical systems—they are the price man has had to pay in order to survive as a social animal without yielding to pure automatism. But a cultural heritage would not, all alone, have been strong or reliable enough to hold up the social structure. That heritage needed a genetic support to provide something essential to the mind. How else account for the fact that in our species the religious phenomenon is invariably at the base of the social structure? How else explain that, throughout the immense variety of our myths, our religions and philosophical ideologies, the same essential 'form' always recurs?'' [28]

There are positive features inherent in most religions. They recognise that the solution to social problems lies in control of the individual as a component vital to future global synergy. They also recognize the immense value of charismatic influential foci, or teachers, in guiding man in the desired direction. For instance, the Christian "Love God and your neighbour" is an aphorism of the synergistic code, as is the Buddhist principle of "harmlessness to all".

Ideally, we should devise synergistic universal codes of education, government and communications practice, but the choice of who should govern this utopian system would seem to be insuperable at present. Moreover man would hardly adhere to the equivalent of a globally acceptable "Hippocratic Oath" for all transactions of human existence.

Since man's mind is a consequence of years of programming by others, man should mature by learning to programme himself. He should realize that he is a slave of language symbols proliferated by his communication systems. He is usually unable to distinguish abstraction from reality. A training scheme as suggested by Korzybski would be an invaluable step in the right direction. [29] Training in the awareness of abstracting would automatically free man of many semantic barriers and enable him to acquire and apply knowledge in a dispassionate way. Further, training in the understanding of how the primitive regions of the brain determine much of man's knowledge and behaviour would pave the way to harmonious living within our physical and mental ecosystems.

A deeper understanding and appreciation of our fellow man could be gained by role-playing the part of the other person. [30] Any person who acts synergistically consciously attempts to experience the other's point of view and thereby refrains from judging him and controlling him by inappropriate standards.

Teaching man to consciously control himself by means of biofeedback or meditation could also be most beneficial to the community as a whole, but institution of such systems depends on the uniform education of significantly large numbers of people in a globally acceptable way. [31]

However, the existence of influential ethical human foci is the most important device for establishing a synergistic society. Just as pacemaking neural foci are vital in maintaining the integrity of the human brain, so human foci are vital in guiding man in a homeostatic direction. The goal of evolution seems to be a global synergistic and intelligent metasocio-mind, so it is essential for concerned human foci to co-ordinate the activities of individual socio-brains. Just as the automatic role of neural foci is to enable the brain to operate at optimum efficiency, so the conscious aim of altruistic human foci should be to understand the phenomenon of mankind and assist every person to realize his fullest potential within the structure of the metasocio-brain.

Governments do not permit the dissemination of ideas contrary to their own, so human foci usually have to operate outside the organization of governments. Their effectiveness nevertheless remains: Consider for example the highly successful religious foci in the form of Jesus, Mohammed and the Buddha.

Many young folk have attempted to solve the problems of existence by "dropping out" from modern society in protest against the direction of evolution of the metasocio-brain, but they usually form other communities at a less evolved and less homeostatic level. Meaningful "dropping-out" should be done in a direction of superior education and increased homeostasis, intended to satisfy the higher needs: Self-actualization and not sheer physical gratification; stimulation of the neural centres which raise man's consciousness to higher human levels and not the lower animal levels.

Parents and educational institutions must teach us to programme and use our neurological equipment scientifically and humanely. The modern call is for freedom, but few of us know the meaning of true freedom which comes with liberation from the mental programmes imprinted in our minds by misguided educators.

Despite our technological sophistication most of us are still primitive organisms, unaware of what the thinking process is, how we are enslaved, brainwashed and programmed by our societies. We are rapidly evolving as prime examples of "unsound minds in unsound bodies".

Man will probably never have a perfect government, so he will have to take steps to avoid being buried in ideologies spread by the communication onslaught. He will have to guard himself against the "graven images" of the mind, the impressiveness of the new communication media, the inherent problems of language abstractions and the limitations of his sensory and neural apparatus.

As integral components of the metasocio-brain we should heed the words of Lilly:

"In the province of connected minds, what the network believes to be true, either is true or becomes true within certain limits to be found experientially and experimentally. These limits are further beliefs to be transcended. In the network's mind there are no limits." [32]

Observation 28: The foundations of a stable noo-ecology lie in the human brain and the use of the technological extensions of our bodies, in particular the mass communication systems.

Observation 29: Religion now has the choice of accepting mutation of its noogenetic information pool or of losing influence to the flood of scientific noogenes.

Observation 30: Man should realize that he is a slave of language symbols proliferated by communication systems and should learn to programme himself constantly in a synergistic manner.

Observation 31: Parents and educators must teach us to programme and use our neurological equipment scientifically and humanely.

Observation 32: True freedom is a consequence of liberation from the mental programmes imprinted in the minds of men by misguided educators.

Observation 33: Just as pacemaking neural foci are vital in maintaining the integrity of the human brain, so altruistic human foci are vital in guiding man towards homeostasis.

Observation 34: The aim of altruistic human foci should be to understand mankind and assist every person to realize his fullest potential within the structure of the metasocio-brain.

Observation 35: "In the network's mind there are no limits" –Lilly.[33]

FOOTNOTES

1. Wiener, N.: quoted by R. Meetham: *Information Retrieval.* Aldus Books, London, 1969, p. 11
2. Johnson, R. A., F. E. Kast and J. E. Rosenzweig: *The Theory and Management of Systems.* McGraw-Hill, Tokyo, 1967, pp. 286-287
3. Nathan, P.: *The Nervous System.* Penguin, Harmondsworth, 1969, p. 215
4. Jorrison, H. J.: "Paleoneurology and the Evolution of Mind:", in *Scientific American.* Jan. 1976, p. 101
5. Jung, C. G. (ed): *Man and His Symbols.* Dell, New York, 1974
6. Ornstein, R. E.: *The Psychology of Consciousness.* W. H. Freeman, San Francisco, 1972, p. 41
7. Payne, B.: *Getting There without Drugs.* Wildwood House, London, 1973, p. 108
8. Mishlove, J.: *The Roots of Consciousness.* Random House, New York/Bookworks, Berkeley, 1975, p. 280
9. ibid. p. 286
10. Taylor, J.: *The Shape of Minds to Come.* Panther, Frogmore, 1974, p. 66
11. Campbell, H. J.: *The Pleasure Areas.* Eyre Methuen, London. 1973
12. Delgado, J. M. R.: *Physical Control of the Mind: Toward a Psychocivilized Society.* Harper and Row, New York, 1970

13. Jung, C. G.: *op. cit.*
14. Thass-Thienemann, T.: *The Interpretation of Language and Understanding the Symbolic Meaning of Language, Vol. 1,* Jason Aronson, New York, 1973, p. 40
15. Richards, W.: "The Fortification Illusions of Migraines," in *Scientific American,* Sept. 1972, pp. 50-51
16. Oster, G.: "Phosphenes", in *Scientific American,* Feb. 1970, p. 83
17. Hubel, D. H.: "The Visual Cortex of the Brain," in *Scientific American,* Nov. 1963, p. 54
18. Stent, G. S.: "Cellular Communication," in *Scientific American,* Sept. 1972, pp. 50-51
19. *ibid.*
20. Gérardin, L.: *Bionics.* World University Library, London, 1968, pp. 10-12
21. *ibid.*
22. Monod, J.: *Chance and Necessity.* Collins Fontana Books, Glasgow, 1974, pp. 154-155
23. Hall, E.: "Your Country Matters," in *Psychology Today* Vol. 2, No. 10, pp. 30-37
24. Dawkins, R.: "Memes and the Evolution of Culture," in *New Scientist.* 28 Oct. 1976, pp. 200-210
25. *ibid.*
26. Andersen P. and S. A. Andersson: *Physiological Basis of the Alpha Rhythm.* Appleton-Century-Crofts, New York, 1968, pp. 13-14
27. Krech, D., R. S. Crutchfield and N. Livson: *Elements of Psychology.* Alfred A. Knopf, New York, 1969, p. 507
28. Monod, J.: *op. cit.* p. 156
29. Korzybski, A.: *Science and Sanity.* The Science Press, Lancaster, Pa, 1941
30. Esser, A. H.: "Synergy and Social Pollution in the Communal Imagery of Mankind'', in J. White (ed.) *Frontiers of Consciousness.* Avon, New York, 1975, p. 351
31. Karlins, M. and L. M. Andrews: *Biofeedback.* Abacus, London, 1975
32. Lilly, J. C.: *The Human Biocomputer.* Abacus, London, 1974, p.xiii
33. *ibid.*

BIBLIOGRAPHY

Lilly, J. C.: *The Human Biocomputer.* Abacus, London, 1974
White, J. (ed): *Frontiers of Consciousness.* Avon, New York, 1975, (in particular Ch. 13)
Koestler, A.: *The Roots of Coincidence.* Picador, London, 1974, (pp. 111-120)
Foster, D.: *The Intelligent Universe.* Abelard, London, 1975
Aronson, E.: *The Social Animal.* The Viking Press, New York, 1972
Rosenfield, A.: *The Second Genesis: the Coming Control of Life.* Vintage Books, New York, 1975
Wooldridge, D. E.: *The Machinery of the Brain.* McGraw-Hill, New York, 1963
Gamson, W. A.: *Simsoc: Simulated Society.* (2nd ed.) Participant's Manual, The Free Press, New York, 1972
Mackay, D. M.: "A Mind's Eye View of the Brain," in Wiener, N. and I. P. Schade (eds.): *Progress in Brain Research. Vol. 17,* Elsevier, Amsterdam, 1965, p. 321
Rorvik, D.: *As Man becomes Machine.* Abacus, London, 1975
Cerminara, G.: *Insights for the Age of Aquarius, A Scientific Analysis of the Problem of Religion.* Prentice-Hall, Englewood Cliffs, N.J., 1973
Korzybski, A.: *Science and Sanity.* The Science Press, Lancaster, Pa., 1941
Gooch, S.: *Total Man.* Abacus, London, 1975
De Ropp, R. S.: *The Master Game.* Picador, London, 1974.
Jung, C. G. (ed.): *Man and his Symbols.* Dell, New York, 1974
Cirlot, J. E.: *A Dictionary of Symbols.* Philosophical Library, New York, 1962

7

The intra-metropolitan communications system

Edward Wilfrid Nassau Mallows *was born in 1905 in England. He obtained a 1st class honours History Tripos in 1926; B.A. (Cantab.) 1927 and an M.A. (Cantab.) 1931. He attended the School of Architecture in London between 1927-1930 and 1932 to 1934, and has obtained various other planning diplomas. He is an Associate of a number of planning and architectural bodies including the Royal Institute of British Architects, Townplanning Institute of Great Britain and was appointed Foreign Affiliate, American Institute of Planners in 1976. Wilfrid was for a number of years senior lecturer, Dept. of Architecture, University of the Witwatersrand. In 1965 he was appointed Professor and Head of Department of Town and Regional Planning. His professional experience is wide and he presently holds the position of Partner in the firm Mallows, Louw, Hoffe and Partners.*

Introduction

". . . the city seems but a model of the brain, with its myriad parts, its communications systems, its structural diversity and lack of overall co-ordination: as if man in creating something outside himself could only copy what was already inside himself, externalizing those patterns and relationships with all their inconsistencies that evolution has saddled him with."

Enlarging on his statement above Mallows writes about the city as a living organism and the townplanner as a surgeon. The townplanner's pen and drawing board are the surgical knife and theatre respectively, the human central nervous system corresponds to the urban communications network, the brain is the central computer and the city is the patient.

In the course of scientific analysis it has become increasingly evident that a major problem confronting social scientists is that the patchy, unsystematic and *ad hoc* basis of research conducted by urban sociologists and other urban scientists has contributed little to urban theory, as has the preoccupation of geographers in describing behaviour in space in the absence of definitive rules of spatial behaviour. Further, the unrealistic assumptions of welfare economists and the emphasis of pure economists on Pareto optimality and economic man has left urban social scientists ill equipped to anticipate the emergence of social dysfunctions and disturbances operative within the social system itself. A pertinent example is the current urban crisis facing many United States cities. Despite large scale research few foresaw the emergence of these social problems.[1]

The above excerpt is perhaps the forerunner of a revolution in communication and urban theory. Many facets of city processes cannot be solved within existing paradigms. Wilfrid Mallows' approach presents a new set of concepts, categories, relationships and methods which may lead to the solution of existing dilemmas while at the same time including relevant aspects of older paradigms. Professor Mallows is rather pessimistic on this point, stating that while the problems of the big city remain, urban scientists will never solve the problems of metropolitan communications. He envisages two solutions, both unacceptable:

- the design of an electronic brain capable of designing cities and their communications systems; and
- genetic engineering to improve levels of ability in man.

Such conclusions should be seen against the ideas postulated in chapters one and three where the authors state that because scientific technology is able to alter the realm of what can be done, the domain of what ought to be done can be defined. Further, the new forms of communication can affect decisions on desirable ends as well as suggesting new means of attaining those ends. The New Rural Society project presented in Chapter 8, describes such trends and deals with the human consequences of reverting to "smaller self-sufficient communities linked by sophisticated communications systems".

Someone once said that civilization is *meeting*[2] people without fighting. This definition pinpoints two basic concepts of urban life: groups meeting, and groups submitting to social control, both complementary to each other and at the root of urban existence. Both concepts would appear to represent for man unnatural activities, not inherent in his makeup – but rather activities which he arrived at with much pain and loss after many millenia of effort.

Ordered urban life of human groups coalescing in one spot to lead a co-operative existence, is a comparitively recent phenomonen in the human story. Probably not much more than 10 000 years in a total span of half a million or a million, however man is defined; this represents between one or two per cent of his past. The major remaining part of his history has not been only non-urban, but non-settled, and probably with less environmental constraint than we can imagine.

The original causation of towns and cities is not in doubt: it was the utilization and processing of excess agricultural production, consequent upon abnormal natural conditions that occurred in the three great river valleys of the Middle East: the Nile, Euphrates, and the Indus. What is interesting is that there may well have been a considerable degree of compulsion by a minority over a majority to start the earliest urban life. Plans that have survived show clearly that earliest towns grew up around and were dominated by great temple and palace complexes. These complexes were run by one elite social group who alone had the necessary know-how to control production by means of written records, systems of land measurement and a precise calendar. Wittvogel[3] has suggested that the traditional oriental despotism originated due to the technical necessity of irrigation control in these valleys, if the surplus of agricultural production was to be maintained. If this is so, the creation of urban life may well have been part of this despotic system and therefore not at all a spontaneous expression of a common human need. Whatever the political and social constraints that were connected with urbanism, the results are not in doubt: a completely new level in environmental control, in knowledge, in material wealth and so in human survival. It is astonishing that today our basic environmental controls – the measurement of time and the measurement of space – are still as originally devised in these earliest settlements.

After 5 000 years, the present human motivation that is still continuing to strengthen the life of cities, is not so easy to define; but it would appear mainly to be the better chances of survival. If men come together in co-operative groups to maximize the use of natural resources – meeting without fighting – then life is better because it is more secure and therefore the danger of scarcity, of poverty, of starvation is further away. The masses of people streaming into cities all over the world seemed to be moved by this simple and basic hope. Our cities, generally much greater in their size and complexity, are serving exactly the same purpose as they did in Sumer of 3000 B.C.

Cities, old and new are linked with a type of social organization usually referred to as civilization, a term which refers to a complex social system which involves its participants in a different set of interactions than do non-civilized societies.[4]

Wilfrid Mallows is concerned with that different set of interactions and their relevance in defining the intra-metropolitan communications system.

K.G.T.

1. Tomaselli, K. G.: "Social Justice: Some Problems at the Interface." *Probe,* 1973-4 pp. 35-38
2. Mallows, E. W. N.: "Urban Planning and the Systems Approach." *Plan,* Feb. 1970, pp. 11-18
3 Wittfogel, K. A.: *Oriental Despotism: A Comparative Study of Total Power.* Yale University Press, New Haven, 1964
4. Gist, N. P. and S. F. Fava: *Urban Society.* Thomas Y. Crowell, New York, 1967, p. 10

The intra-metropolitan communications system

If we are to discuss Metropolitan Communications, we need not only define terms, but also the origin and nature of what the terms represent. The *definitions* are obvious: *metropolitan* pertaining to any large city, say, over 500 000 population; *communications* – any form of transference of goods, ideas or persons between individuals or groups of individuals.

The origins and nature of big cities must be taken as read for the purposes of this chapter: it is the origin and nature of *communications* which need consideration here. Communication of some sort is *common* to all organic life: but human communication has its origin in the human brain and its nature is therefore determined by the structure of the brain, and the way man uses this structure for his individual and social survival. We therefore need to know something about this structure for there is no human communication without some form of mental activity in the first place.

Our knowledge of the brain is still in the exploratory stage, but there seems to be some agreement about its leading characteristics. The first characteristic is that the structure has the complexity of evolutionary growth, and has none of the coherence of something designed. The 10 000 million cells, all more or less similar have in the course of evolution become structured into groups, with a direct group tending to dominate, but with many earlier groupings retained to deal with the simpler basic situations. Nature is very conservative: she keeps the old when superimposing the new. One authority in the United States, Dr. Paul MacLean[1] has postulated that man has not one, but three brains, each superimposed upon the earlier as evolution proceeded, and man's problem is to integrate all three.

According to the MacLean thesis, the *first brain is reptilian*, an inheritance from the age of the reptiles, genetically coded on ancestral memories only and quite unable to adapt to change. Reptiles, being oviparous, have very limited obligations to their offspring, and so, limited need for communication; though some oviparous animals such as birds and insects have gone further and developed fixed societies with very fixed forms of communication, but still no capacity to change. The second brain, the *old mammalian*, is the adjustment needed when animals become viviparous with larger obligations to their offspring and greater demands on territory, food and sex to provide greater permanence to their environment. Hence communication by sound and light and smell became more developed, making possible the formation of social groups. The primates are the great example. The third brain, the *new mammalian,* evolved only with man: it also has a memory and a feed-back system so that it can learn from experience and adjust its future action. This creates a demand for a very wide communication network, to enlarge continually its experience, structure the memory bank and establish external social relationships, all with a view to future use. It is this network which provides language, a social memory, social records and the whole apparatus of knowledge. MacLean however adds: "The greatest language barrier lies between man and his animal brains: the neural machinery simply isn't there for communication in verbal terms".[2] This constitutes a major problem in all human communication systems: language is a strictly limited form of communication. So much then for the first characteristic of the brain, its structural complexity.

The second characteristic is its *inter-connectivity*. Rose, a British writer,[3] says "What matters is not who the cells are but what their address is, who their neighbours are and what their connections are". It is a sophisticated communicaton system between cells that gives the brain what value it has, in spite of the limitations MacLean has outlined, and enables the memory to produce fast results for immediate action.

The third characteristic is a very severe limitation upon this communication system: the brain is *unable to deal with more than a few operations at the same time.* In modern terms, man has a very small "channel capacity": he cannot think or come to decisions on more than 6-7 things at once. To a modern communication engineer this is ludicrously inadequate: Miller[4] states that it is an act of charity to call a man a communication channel at all: compared to a telephone or television he is really only "a bottleneck". It is here that modern communications have added enormously to man's power.

One other limitation of the brain is perhaps worth mentioning— man's inability to form personal relationships beyond groups of 50-100 persons. One writer, Desmond Morris, suggests this is a legacy from the small tribal groups of palaeolithic society, where conditions enforced strict limits to effective social communications. Whatever the reason, man still forms these groups which vitally affect his life and communication needs in big cities and drastically affect the city structure.

The fourth characteristic is a *model-making one*: Oatley[5] says this function is central to the brain – it is an information-processing device which receives, re-codes and transforms information into new models of the external world. These models are creative purposive tools to change the external environment, they are man's peculiar gift, his counterpoise to his channel limitation. Man is a designing animal, but he destroys in order to create, he kills in order to live and the extent of his destructive power is only now becoming fully apparent.

The fifth and last characteristic of the brain is that it is homeostatic, it is self-adjusting to its environment through its feedback system. Human communication is therefore both internal, within itself, and external, with the environment; it is essentially a two-way process, a tool to maintain a dynamic equilibrium between man and his setting.

These five characteristics of the brain give a somewhat uncanny picture when compared to the characteristics of big cities, for the more one considers both, the more the city seems but a model of the brain, with its myriad parts, its communication systems, its structural diversity and lack of overall co-ordination: as if man in creating something outside himself could only copy what was already inside himself, externalizing those patterns and relationships with all their inconsistencies, that evolution had saddled him with.

Whether this is so or not, it is important to realize that when we are discussing metropolitan communications systems, what we are really discussing is the nature of the human brain from which all human societies are derived – including all those very human (or are they animal?) desires, fears, hatreds, pleasures and the rest that drive men on and form the life of human societies, as the Roman satirist Juvenal said long ago.

To make good the defects of his brain man creates communication systems: he forms groups, creates language, keeps records, makes cities. He becomes a political animal and learns the lesson of civilization, meeting without fighting. Artificial extensions enable him to make cities and the communication systems that are their life-blood. Cities become reflections of himself, his limitations, and his efforts to transcend them. He is still limited to his little groups, to his passions for his own, and his hatred of other groups: he still makes models in his mind derived from the most uncertain data which he insists upon imposing on the environment. He still must create and kill in order to create and nothing except *force majeure* seems to stop him.

Two things in particular are reinforced by large cities and their communication systems: the saving of time and the increase in the rate of change, both derived from a rapid change of ideas. It is urban proximity that gives this, as it provides a forcing-house of talent, of the rapid elaboration of new ideas.

There is a correlation between intensity of settlement, individual and social optimization and innovation: it has always been urban communications that have given men freedom to argue, to invent, to create and to change. All over the world men want to come to cities for these reasons, to give themselves a better life.

Generalizations such as those just outlined are however derived from very diverse urban phenomena, caused by the diversity of human groupings and their active systems. For the purposes of this paper I have chosen six such systems: the domestic, the educational, the primary, secondary and tertiary employments and the leisure-culture. Each of these have very different social, economic and cultural constraints and impose very different demands upon any communication system.

The first system, the domestic, is today changing rapidly, with drastic effects upon social patterns. The key change is in the nature of the family as a means of bringing up children. Margaret Mead[6] has suggested the term elective family, which would form elective communities: human groups that have deliberately opted for the rearing of children and designing their lives and settlement systems accordingly. Such communities seem likely to be small in scale, with a need for a high intensity internal communications system for children of all ages to enrich their interaction with one another outside the home and inside and outside the school. They may not be homogeneous: they may include diverse economic and cultural groups which would increase the need for grass roots communication opportunities.

The other side of the domestic system, single people and childless unions, needs the opposite: a high intensity external communication system – a network of contact and physical movement throughout the whole metropolitan area to optimize all their personal friendships.

If Desmond Morris is right, in a city of a million people there may be at least ten to twenty thousand such friendship groups and probably many more since many must overlap one another. All will depend on the communication technology of the city and to the ordinary person the quality of a city is often judged by the quality of the friendships he can make – which means the city is judged by its communication system.

The second system is the educational, the method by which society transmits its values and skills from one generation to the next. These are the first steps away from home and become simulations of later life. Change and conflict become important: new in- and out-groups are formed with strong compulsive norms of their own, with very strong internal communication requirements, often leading to radical social or generation-gap divisions where external communication with other social groups may break down completely leading to violence, gang warfare, crime and a state of what can be called "negative communication". This is one aspect of the need for new institutions to engineer change and to see that the updating and transmission of knowledge can proceed simultaneously, thus ensuring that innovation can take place without violence.

The third, fourth and fifth systems are the primary, secondary and tertiary employments. Primary employment – agriculture and mining – are marginal to the operation of the intra-urban communication system unless food production, such as market gardening, is undertaken within the confines of the metropolitan area.

The secondary employment system, industry, only affects metropolitan communications towards the market end of the long production-consumption chain, but where it does occur it needs strong internal linkages within itself (hence the concept of industrial parks) and strong external linkages in the supply of materials and labour on the one hand and the market on the other. The relationship of the market-orientated industry, the wholesaler and the retailer can become major communication problems because of the importance of time in any market-orientated product.

It is the tertiary employment system, where growth is greatest, that holds the bulk of metropolitan problems. This is the decision-making sector of all developed societies, where fast and accurate information is essential if the use of all resources (human and other) is to be optimized. Moreover the more critical and far reaching the decision, the more the whole nature of man – all his three brains in fact – appear to become involved.

The look of a face, the movement of the eyes, the grasp of a hand, the face-to-face confrontation of a long debate – all these send vital non-verbal messages to the mind when forming decisions, and help to assess the distortions of human motivation and judgment that no communication technology has yet quantified. On these face-to-face, immediate, necessities depend all central business districts, all rush hours. There is however one qualification. It would appear that completely authoritarian regimes, such as the Communist, do not need central business districts and their sophisticated communications systems, since decision-making occurs elsewhere. In the free enterprise society decisions cannot be co-ordinated and made effective unless rapid, often instant, personalized communication channels are available in the central office areas. This would appear the more probable judging by the remarks made by the Moscow delegates at the metropolitan planning conference in Toronto in 1967, where they said they had no use for cities of over 250 000 population and that Moscow and Leningrad were only a historical legacy from the past which they couldn't change. The Japanese delegates in direct contrast said their very big cities such as Tokyo were the life-blood of their economy. Certainly the strongest free enterprise economy, the American, has some of the largest cities, the most intensely developed central office cores, and the most sophisticated communication systems to serve them.

The sixth system is leisure-culture. The growth of time available for non-work in developed economies has created a multitude of new groupings for its use. Many of those activities are survivals of, or reversions to, very old activities of man as if in leisure man returns to his past and the much older parts of his brain, already referred to, take over: hunting, shooting, fishing, swimming, sailing. Even singing, dancing, loving and mating: all have an immense ancestry but often claim more devotion than work. Some of them demand centripetal communications, such as large scale social or tribal celebrations (e.g. football matches), others – the majority – demand centrifugal communications so that the pattern of movement at the week-end becomes the inverse of the pattern of the week. Often the week-end has more intense traffic than the week – no doubt leisure is more important to man than work. What is perhaps more significant is that some leisure has no purpose except immediate enjoyment (e.g. motoring for pleasure without any destination). In such cases quality replaces technical efficiency as a priority and scenic drives are much more important than freeways. Perhaps it will be leisure, not work, that will bring back quality and amenity into our environments.

The effects of all these activity systems upon metropolitan communications are twofold. In the first place it is divisive, it encourages polarization. At the higher end of the economic scale, where the full effect of the communication system can be utilized, the effect is positive, binding all parts into an operational unit, but at the lower end, where only parts of the communication system are available the effect is negative. The absence of telephones, of private, even public transport reduces drastically the choice of work, of leisure, of social relationships, and at the base itself there may be a complete breakdown of communication, with consequent violence and crime. The metropolises take on a pyramidical pattern, which is unified and monolithic at the top, divided and driven apart at its base. Both states are caused largely by the availability, or non-availability of communications.

In the second place, the total effect is one of contrasts: contrasts between the top and bottom but also between high intensity work areas and low intensity leisure areas; contrasts between fast linkages between activity systems and slow pedestrian movements within these systems; contrasts between the different types of human groupings and contrasts between the communication linkages that serve them. In all cases as already stated the quality of metropolitan life, with all those diverse characteristics, depends very largely on the quality, and availabaility, of its communication system.

In conclusion it might be said that we are nowhere near solving the problems of metropolitan communications because we are not near solving the problem of metropolises, of the big cities. It is a problem man has never faced before on the same scale and his brain is displaying some very severe limitations in dealing with it. It may perhaps be that our use of modern technology has outrun our mental capacity to handle its wider, human repercussions. Although man displays a genius at handling mathematical problems and sophisticated machinery, such as computerized traffic control, he is still ignorant of the effects of such technology on human associations, social processes and community groupings. I suspect that there may be a biological ceiling, that only a certain number of able persons are produced every generation and that whereas in pre-industrial societies this ceiling was sufficient for those limited problems, it is quite insufficient for the problems of a mass production, mass consumption, mass communication society. Two solutions are probable, both unacceptable: either the design of an electronic brain capable of designing cities and their communication systems or genetic engineering to improve the levels of ability in any generation. These two approaches may well meet with hostility since man has a built-in resistance to the substitution of totally rational processes for what in the past has been left only to the intuition and imagination. With the complexities of the modern world however, both processes must be integrated somehow.

However unacceptable, some such solutions may be forced on us by the exhaustion of natural resources. If zero growth, zero movement, and zero environmental impact become necessities we may be forced to give up face-to-face contact and rely on remote control, low energy machines for decision-making and revert to much smaller self-sufficient communities linked by sophisticated communication systems. Whatever happens, it seems rapid change is inevitable and this will almost certainly demand redefinition of overall objectives and re-assessment of all our values. Indeed these are underway at the moment, where quality is becoming more important than quantity and some limits are being imposed on human demand which will be in balance with the total environment, both natural and man-made. Thus a lessening demand on quantity will give an opportunity for an increase in quality. If mankind can establish such new values and new approaches it may be able to establish more coherent, more human and more valid metropolitan communication systems.

FOOTNOTES

1. MacLean, P. D.: "Alternative Neural Pathways to Violence". *Alternatives to Violence* (ed. N. Larry), Time-Life Books, New York, 1968, pp. 24-34
2. *ibid.* p. 34
3. Rose, S.: "The Brain in Outline" in *The Brain* (ed. Paterson), BBC, London, 1969
4. Miller, G. A.: *The Psychology of Communication.* Penguin, Harmondsworth, 1969
5. Oatley, K.: *Brain Mechanisms and the Mind.* Thames & Hudson, London, 1972
6. Mead, M.: Interview in *Rand Daily Mail.* 18 July, 1974, p. 12

BIBLIOGRAPHY

Aron, R.: *Progress and Delusion.* Penguin, Harmondsworth, 1972
Ashby, W. R.: *Design for a Brain.* Chapman and Hall, London, 1966
Bertalanffy L. von.: *General Systems Theory: Foundations Development.* Braziller, New York, 1968
Chauvin, R.: *Animal Societies.* Sphere Books, London, 1971
Cherry, C.: *On Human Communication.* M.I.T., Cambridge, 1966
Fein, L. J.: "Ideology and Architecture: Dilemmas of Pluralism" in *Planning for Diversity and Choice* (ed.) S. Anderson, Cambridge, M.I.T. Press, 1968
Hays, H. R.: *From Ape to Angel.* Methuen, London, 1959
Jones, E.: *Towns and Cities.* Oxford University Press, London, 1969
Lessing, L.: "Systems Engineering invades the City". *Fortune,* Jan. 1968, pp. 155-221
McLuhan, M.: *Understanding Media.* New American Library, New York, 1964
Meier, R. L.: *Science and Economic Development.* M.I.T., New York, 1956
Miller, D. R.: *Urban Transportation Policy: New Perspectives.* Heath, Lexington, 1972
Morris, D.: *The Human Zoo.* Jonathan Cape, London, 1969
Mumford, L.: *The City in History.* Secker and Warburg, London, 1961
Newman, O.: *Defensible Space.* Archit. Press, London, 1973, pp. 9-16
Taylor, N.: *The Village in the City.* Temple-Smith, London, 1973
Timms D.: *The Urban Mosaic* Cambridge University Press, Cambridge, 1971
Toffler, A.: *Future Shock.* Pan Books, London, 1970
Walter, W. G.: *The Living Brain.* Penguin, Harmondsworth, 1961
Webber, M. M.: "The Urban Place and the Non-Place Urban Realm," in Webber, M. M. *et al.: Explorations into Urban Structures.* University of Pennsylvania Press, Philadelphia, 1967
Weber, M.: *The City.* The Free Press, London, 1960
Williams R.: *The Land Revolution.* Penguin, Harmondsworth, 1965
Zimmern A.: *The Greek Commonwealth.* Oxford University Press, London, 1961

8

Communications for survival

Peter Goldmark *is President and Director of Research of Goldmark Communication Corporation, Stanford, Connecticut, U.S.A. Previous positions held include President and Director of Research of CBS laboratories and Vice-President of Columbia Broadcasting System Inc. He studied at the University of Berlin and the University of Vienna, where he earned his Ph.D. in Physics.*

Holder of some 160 patents, Peter developed the long-playing record, CCTV and the first practical colour television system. He was responsible for the development of the high resolution readout and ground recording system used in the United States Lunar Orbiter Space Programme.

As Chairman of the National Academy of Engineering on urban problems, he sparkled the New Rural Society Project. He is an active human rights campaigner in his home state.

Bonnie Kraig *is special assistant to Dr. Peter C. Goldmark. Prior to joining G.C.C. in 1972, she was Chairperson of the Task Force on Health and Hospitals for the State Study Commission for New York City, and was responsible for evaluating New York City's hospital and medical care system. Bonnie was at one time an Aide to Mayor John Lindsay of New York City, and had the responsibility for co-ordinating health affairs, and then became Legislative Representative for the Health Services Administration. She has served on lobby groups and has served on many health planning councils. She was also a member of Governor Rockefeller's Committee for Social Problems, and the President's Committee for Health Education.*

Introduction

The conclusions proferred by Mallows in Chapter 7 form the basis of the following contribution, "Communications for Survival". This essay is an outgrowth of the *New Rural Society* (NRS) project which aims to solve the problems of energy utilization, urban congestion and rural-urban migration currently facing the United States.

Observation of these processes have led many researchers to question the historical concept of the city. Max Weber commented that, "The modern city is losing its external and formal structure. Internally it is in a state of decay while the new community represented by the nation everywhere grows at its expense. The age of the city seems to be at an end."[1] Friedman and Millar concur and build upon Weber's statement, "Looking ahead to the next generation, we foresee a new scale of urban living that will extend far beyond existing metropolitan cores and penetrate deeply into the periphery . . . The older established centres, together with the intermetropolitan peripheries that envelop them, will constitute the new ecological unit of America's post-industrial society that will replace traditional concepts of the city and metropolis."[2] This basic element of emerging spatial order is termed the "urban field" and may be viewed as an enlargement of the space for urban living that extends to within commuting boundaries (160 km with present technology) of existing metropolitan areas. In 1965 between 85% and 90% of the total United States population resided in only 35% of the total land area. Consequently Friedman and Millar have discarded the traditional physical, political, economic and demographic criteria usually invoked in definitions of the city. They have likened the city of the future to ". . . a pattern of point locations and connecting flows of people, information, money and commodities".[3] Friedman and Millar contend that:

1. The future growth of population in the United States will occur almost exclusively within areas defined as urban fields.
2. That within each urban field substantial centrifugal forces will propel the settlement of population and location of activities from existing metropolitan centres out into the present periphery.[4]

By 1960 an estimated 150 million Americans lived within urban fields. Friedman and Millar have estimated that by the year 2000, 180 million people will have to be accommodated within roughly the same area. Goldmark is even more pessimistic anticipating a population of 200 million out of a total of 300 million living on less than 10 per cent of total land area.

The NRS project should be seen against this background of increasing urban concentration and also as an attempt to harness anticipated trends in the spread of the urban field in an effort to improve the urban living conditions of United States citizens.

Goals, policies and strategies for regional economic development are aimed at the reduction of regional income disparities, to induce a more balanced regional economic growth through greater integration of the national economy, to reduce growth rates in over-expanded areas and to relieve the poverty of people living in economically distressed areas.

The efforts of the NRS represent only one avenue of research and should be studied in conjunction with other measures such as financial inducements to encourage relocation in the urban peripheries. Growth centre strategies which represent an alternative to the uniform dispersion of investment within chronically depressed areas are equally important. A number of economists have called for the adoption of a national growth centre strategy, whereby development effort would be concentrated in intermediate sized cities which would serve as decentralized centres of economic activity offering employment to those residing in depressed areas.

No one strategy, despite its theoretical soundness, can be considered to be a comprehensive effort in solving the problems of metropolitan areas, for little detailed empirical research has yet been conducted. The NRS, however, realized this limitation and have set in motion a vast programme of empirical research.

The NRS project has as its basic aims:

1. The application of existing and new communications technologies to improve the quality of life for people in rural communities in the United States.
2. To give all Americans the opportunity to work and live in small attractive rural communities.
3. To put everyone in contact with everyone else within the city through telephone, AM-FM radio and television broadcasting through broadband cables carrying a multitude of TV channels into individual homes and a second broadband cable system inter-connecting the major public institutions. External communications services will connect business, industry and government with their operations in other cities through telephone, videophone and other telecommunications facilities.
4. Social considerations include the maintenance of adequate interpersonal communication despite distance constraints and research into the acceptability of new forms of electronic communications systems to potential users.

The underlying assumptions of the project are:

- That by the year 2000 at least 50 million people already in cities may wish to be part of the new rural society.
- That all the necessary inventions have already been made and that broadband communications systems can now be imaginatively applied to the needs of business, government, education, health care and cultural pursuits to stimulate development of the new rural society.

Already Peter C. Goldmark, the NRS project director, is urging public action to encourage dispersal. Recent advances in communications technology, he argues, will overcome the distance constraints which previously prevented decentralization.

Although this paper, unlike those which precede it, is almost entirely geared to an overview of specific NRS studies we feel that its significance lies predominantly in its efforts to combine theory with pragmatic action. At least one of the futuristic communications technologies mentioned in Chapter One will be operating in The United States by the end of 1976 and others have already been designed. "Communications for Survival" represents a challenge to the conclusion offered in Chapter 5 where the author states, "There is some doubt whether new telecommunications media will have sufficient power to offset centralizing forces." Nevertheless, the ultimate form of the NRS would be the aspatial city described in Chapter 5, with its man/machine relationships and the inherent danger of man becoming subservient to his electronic inventions.

The basic tenet of "Communications for Survival" then, is the analysis of ways in which real income (access to society's scarce resources) may be redistributed in rural areas in an effort to resolve the urban, rural and energy crises which will face the United States by the year 2000.

K.G.T.

1. Weber, M. *The City*. Free Press, New York, 1958, p. 62
2. Friedman, J. & J. Miller: "The Urban Field". in *Journal of the American Institute of Planners,* Vol. 31, No. 4, 1965, pp. 312-319
3. ibid.
4. ibid.

Communications for survival

The last two centuries stand out in history as a triumph for science and technology, but mankind has not always benefited. Many scientists have been so involved in their own disciplines that they have tended to overlook the true needs facing society, and it is evident that scientists face a responsibility and a challenge which cannot go unheeded. An attempt should be made to apply at least a fraction of our diverse talents and education in solving the major problems presently facing society, problems which fall into the categories urban, rural and energy.

At the turn of the century, one third of the United States population lived in urban areas, while the remaining two thirds resided in rural parts of the country. A mounting migration reversed these percentages to the present population distribution of three quarters urban (and suburban) and one quarter rural. Urban centres expanded rapidly to accommodate the population growth, and led to countless unprecedented social, economic and environmental problems.

Concurrently, the quality of life in rural areas began to decline and was unable to compete with the real or imagined attractions of urban life. Concomitant with the onset of the urban and rural problems, was the accelerated exhaustion of traditional sources of energy supply.

The urban problem

If crime can be considered an index of social dysfunction, then urban areas contrast alarmingly with rural. Fifteen times more street robberies per unit population occur in a city of one million than in a town of ten thousand.

Other relevant indexes, for example, pollution levels, traffic congestion and health standards are all signs of a population saturation which urban scientists are unable to deal with adequately.

Many people and businesses have opted for a suburban location to escape urban problems. This trend has expanded the boundaries of urban areas, and placed an additional strain on existing facilities which may ultimately impair the quality of suburban life as well.

The rural problem

Unfavourable psychological attitudes towards rural regions are the cause of emigration of young, talented and energetic people who rove in search of higher incomes, better community services, and more job opportunities.

The energy problem

Parallel to this unplanned population dislocation has been an indiscriminate use of energy resources, particularly with regard to oil consumed during daily commuting (about 33% of the total oil consumption).

The first major concerted effort to apply science and technology, and in particular communications disciplines to national problems took place in 1971 under the auspices of the National Academy of Engineering's Committee on Telecommunications.[1] Its proposal was the New Rural Society project. The objective was to apply telecommunications technology to ease the plight of the cities by upgrading the quality of life in rural communities. Conditions were to be established whereby a voluntary decentralization of people, business and government would occur, which would contribute to a control and amelioration of the urban and energy crises.

Overview of specific studies and experiments pursued by the new rural society to date

The New Rural Society (NRS) project was funded under a grant from the Department of Housing and Urban Development and the Department of Transportation, both under a contract to Fairfield University, Connecticut.

Since 1974, a broad study has been made of the historical role of science, technology and telecommunications as a tool to aid in solving social problems. Also, a number of specific studies (employment, health care, community interaction, teleconferencing, etc.) were conducted, together with actual tests and pilot operations.

NRS has identified five areas considered critical to the development of viable rural communities and where communications technology could make a significant contribution. These are:

1. employment;
2. health care;
3. continuing education and vocational training;
4. entertainment and cultural opportunities; and
5. community interaction and planning.

Employment

One of the major objectives is to create job opportunities in rural areas to retain people who might otherwise leave and to attract new residents from congested areas. Urban business considering decentralization to rural areas requires assurance that such a move will be a cost-effective operation. Organizations are often concerned that relocation may be more dependent on and raise the cost of their communication activities, consume more employee time, cause delays or even the loss of essential contracts. NRS contends that these problems may be overcome in most cases by proper planning and suitable application of existing telecommunications technologies. To provide a basis for this planning, NRS tested its communications audit technique with several of the state of Connecticut's criminal justice agencies.[2]

The purpose of the audit is to establish the general and external communications processes and requirements of an organization and to show how reliance upon travel and complex communications systems might be minimized. Once an organization's communications patterns have been established and analyzed, it is possible to plan for changes that would make them more effective and identify organizational components which could be relocated most easily to a rural area by virtue of their communications requirements.

Effort has also been devoted to the study and design of an electronic system that could serve as a satisfactory alternative to face-to-face business conferences in decentralized government and private organizations.

A field trial of the NRS audio-teleconferencing system by the Union Trust Company Bank of Connecticut showed the system to be a highly useful, well-utilized technique for conducting regular meetings between bank executives in two cities. The teleconference system was judged a favourable alternative to travel for most meetings and led to more effective time utilization. The monthly cost associated with teleconferencing (depreciation of equipment and monthly charges for telephone line) represented only 50 percent of what the Bank would have had to spend for transportation and executive time if the same number of meetings had been conducted on a face-to-face basis.[3]

Health care

Access to essential health care services is commonly not available to rural communities. Of all rural and small town respondents, one third ranked health problems on a par with, or even slightly above income as their primary personal concern (sufficient income does not guarantee rural residents adequate medical services).

Physicians tend to settle in urban or suburban places because their families, like three-quarters of the American population, prefer the amenities offered there. About one third of all U.S. doctors have chosen to work in research laboratories, industry, public health, academic faculties or to serve as hospital administrators, and the proportion of physicians who meet the primary care needs of patients on a continuing basis, has been diminishing.

The trend towards increasing specialization and the concentration of doctors in metropolitan centres has served to deprive many rural communities of adequate health care. Although the total number of U.S. physicians has increased 28% during the past decade, the proportion in general practice has dwindled sharply.[4]

The NRS project therefore aims to improve the quality of services in rural areas. It is believed that a systems approach is the best way to achieve good care and effective cost control. Here emphasis is on prevention, early diagnosis, less costly care and continuing patient and doctor learning opportunities, rather than on hospital and nursing home care.

Community interaction and planning

The separation of job from residence, among others, has made it difficult to realize a high degree of community interaction and planning. Today's average individual moves around more than ever before and plays many roles. Under these circumstances, different communities may have different interests. This makes it difficult to define the term community precisely. A definition that would probably prove acceptable to most scholars, however, is that: "A community consists of persons in social interaction within a geographic area and having one or more additional common ties."[5]

There is an idea that contemporary social organization has been destroying some of the more meaningful human associations and values that small town residents have traditionally acquired in church, family and neighbourhood.[6]

When people do not live and work in the same location, they may be less inclined to involve themselves in community affairs. Similarly, working parents who travel long distances to their jobs may have very little time during the week to spend with their families.

Much thought has been given to the problem of how to reclaim a sense of community. We believe that if people live and work in the same town, they are apt to become involved in local affairs and to develop community commitments. In addition, a focal point for community activities needs to be established in order to encourage citizen participation. This approach has proved most useful where activities have emerged from real needs identified by the residents of the town. A survey indicated that the greatest interest was in continuing education opportunities and improved public services.

Potentially, a centre can foster community interaction by offering a variety of cultural and educational activities and by providing a forum for debating important public issues.

Transportation

Under contract to the U.S. Department of Transportation the NRS will:

- investigate the implications for transportation technology of the redistribution of population to non-metropolitan areas;
- determine how and under what circumstances telecommunications might constitute an acceptable alternative to the movement of people and goods;
- define the complementarity of transportation and telecommunications in stimulating rural economic development and growth;
- propose planning considerations which would help local government officials and citizens in rural areas to plan more effectively for the improvement and development of their area.

Although the NRS identifies five dimensions to the quality of life, the current study focuses on the most basic of these, employment. Two rural counties (Indiana, Pennsylvania and Pitt, North Carolina) selected as study sites have yielded detailed economic, educational, medical and social data profiles. The project is using an econometric forecasting model to project the economic impact of changes expected in the industrial environments of the two sites. The model is also able to predict the effect of transportation improvements on industrial output, employment, income and population, as well as pollution levels and energy use. Communication indices, incorporated into the model, will assist an assessment of the impact of communications improvements. The hypothesis that greater percentages of the U.S. economy will become information and service orientated, leads to the conclusion that accessibility through telecommunications will be more important than accessibility through transportation. Applications of these two technologies to enhance the quality of life for current and future residents of the counties will be investigated.

Implementation, general considerations

A full implementation of the NRS plan is tantamount to setting a new national goal. Its aim is to optimize the match between population distribution and available human, environmental and energy resources to be independent of imports and assure a high quality of life for all Americans in the future. Experience with the NRS project has shown that this goal could be reached by the end of this century if the problem were divided into smaller, manageable units. Making decentralization a goal within each of the 50 states, would come close to accomplishing this purpose. There are a number of states on the Eastern and Western Seaboards where the population density is already so high that effective relief could only be derived from making migration to less densely populated states desirable. In order to alleviate the urban problems, the poor and minority groups should be able to decentralize first. For the many low-populated and economically underdeveloped regions of this country, self-planning has to come to grips with the fact that economic growth, through a decentralization of business and government, will require accepting a limited amount of immigration to fill the new jobs and will have to provide for residents seeking employment. Where the states represent the natural individual decentralization units, there is the advantage that they are largely self-contained politically and administratively, and most of them have sufficient resources necessary to accomplish the desired goals. The development of rural regions can best be achieved by optimizing the interchange of existing resources in a given area between an economically developed focal centre and its less developed surroundings. An example would be short distance commuting to a manufacturing and business centre from a surrounding rural area which is attractive and has adequate health care, access to continuing and vocational education, cultural and recreational activities, and social interaction. Federal co-ordination of state efforts is necessary, especially in terms of transportation and communication. Redistribution would not only involve decentralization of business and industry but of federal and state government operations. As a result, government would be more responsive to local needs. It is unfortunate that no single federal agency has the charter to cope with the solutions proposed by the NRS project, since federal co-operation is needed to provide a sufficiently funded and well co-ordinated effort.

Proposals for specific projects

Transportation

The redistribution of people from large urban centres to rural areas would have to be stimulated by a decentralization of government and business operations. It has been argued that transportation links between rural areas and a larger population centre disproportionately favour the larger community. There is good reason to believe that, since the use of communications systems overcomes separation and minimizes movement, the effects on growth may favour the smaller communities. This could have major significance for the relative investments between transportation and communications, where the issue is to strengthen rural communities in terms of quality of life as defined by the community. The Department of Transportation is thus facing decisions which may require it to embrace telecommunications as an integral part of transportation planning. Considerations regarding mass transportation versus individual personal travel partially substituted by telecommunications, when superimposed on a system of rebalanced population distribution, can only be planned optimally when both technologies are fully applied. In order to improve the quality of life in the U.S. rapidly and at minimum energy cost a replication of the optimized subregional systems within individual states should be the immediate goal.

NRS proposes to do the following:

1. Broaden and refine the techniques now under development for measuring the influence of communications on the economy of rural regions. The Harris Econometric Model would be extended towards modelling the means by which telecommunications can affect the development of focal economic points, and the largest surrounding region.[7] The communications indices will measure the impact of mass media, as well as modes of industrial communications, such as data handling. The indices would embrace the use of specific communications technologies needed for maximizing government and service employment, and to extending their influence on surrounding rural areas in terms of improved health, educational and cultural services. The complementary roles of transportation and telecommunications are essential ingredients in these analyses.

2. Certain institutional problems have to be considered:

   (a) Which government, business or civic organizations will be affected by the processes outlined under 1., and what legal, legislative or public educational programmes need to be developed to ease the enactment of necessary changes?

   (b) Which institutions and what methods need to be involved in the necessary long-range planning functions and which stimuli have to be provided for individuals to participate in such activities within their communities?

   (c) What institutional barriers need to be removed to arrive at a transportation and communication system best able to achieve the desired goal in the region?

3. Local work centres can effect a major influence on the balance between transportation and communication and on energy usage in the proposed rural models. Equipped with communication and office facilities, these centres permit employees to travel to the larger industrial locations less often, and only when face-to-face meetings or conferences are required. At other times contacts and correspondence could be concentrated into certain days, and travel reduced.

Urban needs

The impact of a voluntary population distribution will lead to what may be called a Headquarters City, where the headquarters of business, commerce, the arts and sciences, of medicine and education are located. This is already the case in several of our large cities. The numerous divisions, services and subsidiaries of these headquarters operations could be dispersed throughout the respective state.

A voluntary metropolitan decentralization must become a national goal and the creation of rural employment opportunities through telecommunications is essential for urban residents who are now unemployed or underemployed. Job training would be geared to the underprivileged people who would be migrating to the rural areas from the city and to residents in rural areas. In addition to job training, there must be a state and federal commitment to provide the opportunity to resettle, and assure employment in the place of destination. It is estimated that expenditures would be a fraction of what the city now spends directly and indirectly on welfare provision.

The opportunity for minorities and poor people to transfer with their families into attractive rural communities represents a vital step towards improving the quality of life for this sizeable segment of the population.

The growth control of a community, including the type of employment and the increase in population that are acceptable, should be based upon local planning, with public participation, and co-ordinated with overall regional and state objectives. The decentralization of government (state and federal) and the extent to which it reduces the operating costs of planning and administrative agencies is an important part of an overall distribution plan. NRS proposes to develop criteria to test, measure and evaluate the effectiveness of decentralized government operations in sociological and economic terms using its communications audit technique. An assessment of the various forms of communications technology, and their substitutability for travel would be part of the same study.

Health care services

Research has indicated that, when education is made relevant to the health requirements of individuals and their families, it can produce significant improvement in their actions. As a consequence, people are able to react to health problems with more knowledge and confidence, and thereby reduce the need for expensive clinic and hospital facilities and services.

To educate people in home health care on a wide scale, they should be reached near to where they live and work and be able to follow a schedule most suitable to their needs. A new electronic delivery system for learning called RTS (Rapid Transmission and Storage) has been developed for use in learning centres and would be employed in the proposed project. The low cost, high quality and flexibility of the recorded programmes make this a cost-effective way to apply health education across the country.

NRS proposes a programme in which clinics, manned by physician assistants, would be set up in the various townships, readily accessible to the residents. Based upon tests and experiences thus far, the majority of cases can be handled by physician assistants. In the remaining instances, a supervising physician in attendance will be able to advise and assist through telecommunication links, interconnecting these clinics to a nearby hospital.

Adult and vocational education

Ever since the invention of the printing press, the primary means for transferring knowledge has been the instructor and the printed word. Today, in a world of ever accelerating change, it is necessary to improve the process of learning. This is especially important in view of the fact that one quarter of our population has not completed high school, and some twenty percent of all adults want to learn some subject of their choosing – academic, vocational, home and hobby related, etc.

Educational institutions traditionally serve only those who come to the campus and it has been recognized only recently that a great many people would like to learn near where they live or work. Community colleges, of which there are some 1 200, business and industry are aware of this challenge.

Community colleges today are faced with more people wanting to learn more subjects in off-campus learning centres than can presently be satisfied. It is not economically feasible to send instructors to learning centres near where people live to teach all the subjects desired, and still retain schedule flexibility at reasonable cost to the user. To meet such needs, educators and scientists have, for the first time, combined to develop a method of learning and delivery. The RTS system integrates the best available educational and technology resources into a universal system and went into operation with a group of community colleges during the latter half of 1976.

The following characterizes the RTS system:

1. Up to 30 one-hour, or 60 half-hour or 120 fifteen-minute programmes, etc. can be stored on a one-hour standard 1″ video cassette. Up to 30 of these can be shown simultaneously in as many classrooms. This satisfies the requirement of continuous enrolment, whereby people can start a new semester on any subject each week, or every other week, etc, to suit their own schedules.
2. Sound is the main medium and is illustrated with picture and graphics material. Illustrations are synchronized with the corresponding words to create a single impact on the student.
3. Motion is provided only when essential, for clarification or emphasis.
4. A wide choice of learning materials can be produced quickly and at low cost – a fraction of conventional video or motion picture presentation.
5. Programmes can be stored on 1″ video cassettes or transmitted over standard television stations, cable links, or microwave systems.
6. Updating pictures and sound is an easy process and worldwide use is possible through dubbing the sound track.
7. Printed materials are provided with RTS in the form of texts, administrative guide, and testing aids. It is possible to arrange the programmes so that each lesson has built-in testing sections, an important factor in any successful learning programme.

Postal service in rural areas

In order to upgrade rural mail and message delivery the NRS programme will suggest the following:

1. *Examination of issues on state-by-state basis*
    (a) Determination of maximum ranges in delivery time between central collection points and outlying post offices of various districts (especially in remote areas).
    (b) Availability of preferable collection points in adjacent states.
    (c) Percentage of various classes of mail destined to different regions of the world, particularly rural areas.
    (d) The degree of privacy desired for various classes of mail and type of mail or messages on which to focus initially.
    (e) Consider two-way terminals designed for these specific services, located at all distant and particularly remote post offices, utilizing

alpha-numeric printout, with digital signals on standard phone lines. This could be utilized primarily at night-time (estimated capacity – 10 000 pages, averaging 500 words each, per terminal between 6 p.m. and 8 a.m.)

For the transmission of documents, drawings, handwritten messages, etc. a portion of the night schedule may be devoted to facsimile with highest efficiency utilization of telephone circuits (maximum two minutes per page.)

(f) Investigations of optimum delivery system for new service between remote post office and addresses.

2. *Equipment considerations for this system*
   (a) Availability or adaptation of existing devices or systems.
   (b) Cost of hardware and of operation.
   (c) Degree of automation.

3. *Delivery of electronic messages from post office to distant addresses via TV or telephone, or both or other alternatives.*

4. *Interstate and intrastate regulations, as well as telephone system interconnections.*

5. *Investigation of potential users of the rural mail or message system*
   (a) Government agencies – local, state, federal.
   (b) Business and industry.
   (c) Hospitals, laboratories, physicians' offices, etc.
   (d) Law enforcement.
   (e) Schools, libraries, etc.

6. *Proposal for specific pilot operations in selected states and regions, and their relationships with other NRS projects planned for the same places.*

7. *Implementation plan for full project activity, including cost, duration, and anticipated results.*

Environmental protection

A decentralized population pattern can have profound effects on environmental regulations and their influence on the country's economy. The dispersion of power plants and automobile travel as a result of more even distribution of people in the metropolitan and rural communities will result in less air and water pollution and should be more easily controlled on a local level.

The impact of telecommunications on living conditions and transportation is an important factor in voluntary dispersal of people and jobs, and is expected to result in significant easing of environmental constraints.

ENERGY

Energy was not an issue when early in this century two thirds of all Americans lived in rural communities.

Pollution and almost total reliance on oil for electricity and transportation assumed crisis proportions when migration from rural areas resulted in three-quarters of the population living and working in metropolitan regions.

It is proposed to develop conditions for an optimal match between population distribution and the most efficient use of our energy resources. If a greater proportion of the population lived and worked according to a decentralized pattern, power generation could be dispersed as well.

Calculations based on available data indicate that one third of gasoline consumption is due to cars being driven daily to and from work in our large metropolitan centres. Thus an examination of this nation's energy utilization based on current life patterns and a comparison with alternative modes of population distribution are likely to show that we may be able to attain reliance solely on our own energy resources for centuries to come and at the same time maintain a high quality of life. This would permit us to develop alternate sources of energy without haste and undue burden on our economy.

Communication services

Communications technology is a crucial factor in providing rural communities with the necessary services to make them viable alternatives to urban life. However, there still remains a sizeable portion of our rural population without access to an adequate TV broadcast service.

An even larger fraction have virtually no cultural and recreational opportunities available to them.

It is unfortunate that the notion "Wired Nation" was created, giving the impression that all of rural America can be made accessible by means of cable TV. To provide all rural homes with an adequate cable TV service would create an enormous economic strain, and regulatory problems of enormous magnitude.

At the NAE-NASA 1974 Summer Study, a broadcast satellite system "Rural-Sat" was recommended which required a modest investment by the users, and could make adequate broadcast services available to all rural residents.

"Rural-Sat" consists of a pair of special communication satellites in synchronous orbit over the equator in such a way as to cover the US optimally. The basic role of the "Rural-Sat" System is to serve all rural homes, whether in communities or on farms. It will perform three types of broadcast services:

1. A national coverage capable of being received in any home, but especially rural homes.
2. Regional broadcast programmes each covering approximately one-quarter of the U.S. corresponding to the time zones.
3. A new high-resolution colour TV broadcast system for theatre projection anywhere in the country, of live cultural events, such as theatre, opera, ballet, museums, conventions, etc.

In the following the technical description and details of the Rural-Sat System are given as published by the National Academy of Sciences at the end of 1975 from the Panel on Uses of Communication to the Space Applications Board of the Assembly of Engineering, National Research Council.

CONCEPT FOR A NATIONWIDE SATELLITE COMMUNICATIONS SYSTEM TO SERVE RURAL AREAS

To fulfil the need to make rural America attractive for more people and to deliver to the home continuing vocational and health education as well as regional and community information, in addition to the entertainment and public affairs offerings on national TV, the Panel offers a concept of a synchronous communications satellite system consisting of two identical satellites, each with fourteen 40 MHz TV transponders each with 100 watts output. Typically, the total of 28 transponders can be utilized as follows. On Satellite I, three 400 watt high-power signals are produced by combining 4 output stages for each of three national TV channels corresponding to the commercial networks. These three TV signals, each 40 MHz wide, are fed to the same antenna, covering the entire US. Two more channels on the same satellite serve regions I and II, approximately corresponding to Time Zones I and II, counting from the West. Satellite II has two national broadcast channels, again each combining the output from four 100 watt transmitters. One of these channels could be assigned to the Public Broadcast Service and the other to cable networking or for educational-health care services. Of the remaining six 100 watt transmitters, two serve Time Zone III and four broadcast to Time Zone IV (East Coast of the U.S.) This makes it possible on the average for 6 states to share one transponder. Thus, within a given region or time zone, each state can have a one sixth share of a broadcast day to transmit pertinent, local or regional information which can be received everywhere within the zone. Each satellite would have two antennas, the smaller one taking the broadcast feeds covering the entire nation, and the large antenna serving the individual zones.

Figure I illustrates the above and also the number of 40 MHz channels transmitted by the two satellites. The twelfth 40 MHz channel, namely F6, is reserved to be combined with F5 providing an 80 MHz wide special broadcast channel for the high-resolution colour TV signals for theatre projection discussed under ''Teleculture''.

Regarding reception, it is estimated that a two-metre antenna, together with a 250° receiver and using a parametric amplifier at room temperature, will provide commercially acceptable pictures anywhere in the U.S.

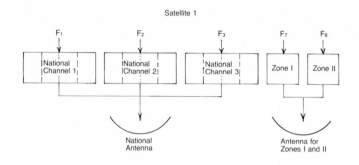

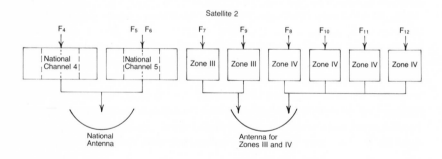

Figure 1

In addition to this primary mission, the Rural-Sat can perform a number of other functions to fill rural needs, such as electronic mail and educational and health services. These are described in detail below:

1. The use of the Rural-Sat as a main communication link for electronic mail

The Rural-Sat system provides a double bandwidth channel for the high-resolution theatre TV service. Assuming that the use of this extra wideband channel for broadcasting of live cultural events is averaging four hours per 24 hour day, then the channel could be used 20 hours per day for relaying electronic mail. Augmenting this with a partial use of the regional channels for mail-service, one could realize the equivalent of a full 24 hour use each day with an 8 MHz video band and 80 MHz RF channel. This could handle yearly 2,5 billion pieces of mail (single page.) Based on a surcharge of 50c per page for satellite mail, the yearly income generated would be one and a quarter billion dollars. Because of the low cost of the receiving terminals, every post office in the U.S., including the smallest rural ones could afford a receiving station. At the same time many businesses, government agencies, institutions, etc. could receive electronic mail directly from the satellites only a fraction of a second after it was transmitted from the ground-station nearest to the collection centre. Appropriate coding techniques will assure necessary privacy. A ground network is required for forwarding electronic mail from a given region's post offices to a ground station which then transmits it to the Rural-Sat. Postal stations serving small communities or low density areas will only require narrow band (conventional telephone) or 48 kHz lines to intermediate post offices from where signals are speeded up and forwarded over broadband links to the nearest ground station. Businesses and government operations with high mail traffic would have direct links to and from the nearest post office thus bypassing local processing. It is important to stress that the complexity of a national electronic mail system rests not only in the satellite collection and distribution system, but more so in the high-speed paper handling and scanning equipment located in a large number of post offices all over the country. The magnitude of such installations will depend on the amount of traffic flowing through the particular post office which is also the determinant for the bandwidth of the communication channel feeding out of that postal office. Slow-speed paper handling and electronic scanning equipment would be less complex and also less expensive.

2. National and regional educational services

A new type of instructional service is described, using the Rural-Sat system at night-time, when most TV transmitters are normally off the air. The new learning format and technology, which permits a highly compressed transmission and storage of lessons of any length, based on a carefully composed sound and still-picture presentation, and using motion only when necessary, has been developed and is available for the Rural-Sat. If we assume the use of one pair of satellites (5 national and 8 regional channels), then one national channel could be employed together with the 8 regional channels for seven hours of night transmissions (one hour of the total of eight night hours would be reserved for augmenting the postal service as described previously under 1). The educational programmes would be divided into the following categories:

- *Supplementary audio-visual material for:*
  Primary and secondary schools.

- *Complete courses for:*
  Continuing adult education, with or without college credits.
  Vocational and job improvement.
  Professional education for physicians, lawyers, scientists, etc.
  Health care for residents.
  Home care, etc.

Existing learning centres would be used nationally, employing receiving equipment low enough in cost to permit widest distribution. Such learning centres in rural communities or cities, would be in churches, schools, libraries, hospitals, prisons, community centres, etc. and the course recorded at night-time would be stored for the next day's classes.

One national and eight regional channels together can transmit close to 2 000 different half-hour lessons each night. The eight regional channels could be shared nightly by each of the 48 states permitting each state to transmit 42 of its own programmes. It should be noted that the transmissions by each state within a zone could be received by all of the region's population. Thus, various states could co-ordinate their programmes so as to mimimize duplication and jointly provide the maximum choice.

Curricula

An entirely new, comprehensive health programme is proposed, which takes advantage of the RTS format and delivery system.

The new service for physicians and allied health manpower would be provided at the local hospital or other health facility.

1. *Physician information*

As a result of their heavy work schedules, doctors do not have an opportunity to study the wealth of material published related to the uses of certain drugs, and their relationship to various diseases, etc. Often, unwittingly, a physician errs in prescribing certain medication, and the outcome can be serious.

It is suggested that jointly with one or more pharmaceutical houses, programmes be developed that focus upon the uses and abuses of pharmaceuticals and drugs. These mini-courses would not substitute for medical representatives, but rather would support their efforts, by re-inforcing and sharpening the information content in the literature. Stress would be upon the advantages of certain pharmacological aids, research underway and so on.

2. *Physician continuing education and re-certification*
As part of the same philosophy, course material would provide continuously updated information regarding particular fields of interest, such as internal medicine, allergy, paediatrics, etc.

3. *Nurses and allied health personpower*
Programmes would be developed to provide information concerning the work of the nurses – including regulations and legislation affecting that profession – as well as course material to encourage career opportunity for medical technicians and other support people.

The ability of the RTS system to transmit a wide variety of programmes at night means that it lends itself especially well to the Rural-Sat proposal. The capacity to select from a vast range of courses is central to the success of the system.

In summary, the Rural-Sat system proposed will make it possible to provide rural communities with components necessary for a viable life style.

NRS ABSTRACTS

"Experiments and field tests of communications systems"

"Laboratory Communications Experiments." *NRS Reference 301,* May 1973

Because of the difficulty of providing video links at reasonable cost, three experiments were undertaken to evaluate different types of audio-only conferencing systems. The hypothesis that multichannel audio would be more acceptable than a monaural system for two-person exchanges, because of the greater realism and richness of sound such a system affords, was not supported (Experiment I). However, the hypothesis that a multispeaker (one loudspeaker for each person) audio-only system would have advantages compared with a monaural system for group conferencing was supported (Experiment II). The major advantages and disadvantages of a two-speaker sound system which creates a distinct sound source for each conference participant was explored in greater detail in Experiment III. The analysis suggested that this system had four main advantages over a monaural system. It was seen by users as (a) providing separate sound images for the different conferees, thus facilitating speaker-identification and possibly giving a greater sense of individuality to the conferees, (b) facilitating a better, more stimulating discussion, (c) apparently resulting in a better overall sound quality, and (d) facilitating a warmer, more personal contact between the conferees.

It is concluded that audio-only teleconferencing is acceptable in more situations than has been thought previously and that more research should be devoted to this type of teleconferencing than has been the case in the past.

"An NRS Project Experiment to Determine the Effects of Acquaintance and Communication Medium in a Bargaining Task" *NRS Reference 302,* May 1974

An acquaintance hypothesis is proposed which in its general form maintains that there is an interaction between the degree to which people are acquainted and their ability to communicate over different types of communication systems.

The basic premise in this experiment is that uncertainty is uncomfortable and that efforts will be made to eliminate it. The concept of uncertainty can be applied both to the relationship between people and to the characteristics of communications systems. It would follow that between individuals becoming acquainted reduces uncertainty. An audio communications system can be said to impose more uncertainty on a contact than a face-to-face meeting, because it does not provide any visual information. Individuals using an audio system would be better off if they were acquainted (have low interpersonal uncertainty) than otherwise. It is also possible that where uncertainty between people is low, that a face-to-face meeting is unnecessary and counterproductive, because it involves redundant information. Thus a face-to-face meeting between acquaintances would be less fruitful than the same type of meeting for non-acquaintances. These considerations underlie the following hypotheses:

1. Using an audio-only system (high uncertainty), acquainted persons would perform a problem-solving communication task significantly better than would unacquainted persons.
2. Conversely, in a face-to-face meeting (low uncertainty), unacquainted persons would perform the task better than acquainted persons.

Eighty-eight subjects were tested in a 2 × 2 randomized factorial design; subjects were either strangers or acquaintances, and met via either an audio system or face-to-face. The communication task was to develop a priority ordering of a number of topics by sharing information. Subjects met for five minutes and then were given the evaluation questionnaires.

The experimental results supported both hypotheses.

"An NRS Project Experiment to Determine the Effects of Acquaintance and Communication Medium in a Bargaining Task." *NRS Reference 303,* September 1974

NRS found in an experiment dealing with the acquaintance hypothesis that acquainted people performed a problem solving/decision making task significantly better than unacquainted people using an audio-only communication medium.

The purpose of this experiment was to extend the scope of the acquaintance investigation to a bargaining task. In relation to problem solving, bargaining tends to involve more personal conflict and, therefore, is more difficult to perform over a communications system than face-to-face. The following hypotheses were investigated.

1. Using an audio-only system (high uncertainty), acquainted persons would perform a bargaining communication task significantly better than would unacquainted persons
2. Conversely, in face-to-face meeting (low uncertainty), unacquainted persons would perform the task better than acquainted persons.

Forty subjects were tested in a 2 × 2 randomized factorial design; subjects were either strangers or acquaintances, and met via either an audio system or face-to-face. The communication task was to develop a compromise strategy based on two conflicting strategies. Subjects met for ten minutes and then were given the evaluation questionnaires.

The main hypotheses were not supported.

Further analysis of the bargaining results revealed that the participants' strategy in bargaining was to compromise. This was true in all the experimental conditions except where unacquainted persons used an audio system. In this condition, the stronger case dominated.

Communicating by audio seems to minimize the non-task specific factors which would affect the outcome of a bargaining task. In this latter experimental condition, the participants had no prior knowledge about each other and no visual information. Thus the inherent strength of their bargaining positions became more decisive and was less affected by other considerations such as status.

"Broadband Teleconference Test Between Hartford and Willimantic" *NRS Reference 304,* January 1973

A field test of teleconferencing was conducted for a two-day period between Hartford and Willimantic. The aims were:
- to provide a two-day demonstration of teleconferencing service between two locations separated by a significant physical distance.
- to design the teleconference facilities in light of the laboratory results.
- to arrange for real business to be transacted using these facilities.
- to expose all groups of conferees to two different types of teleconferencing systems, one of which would require broadband transmission and the other of which could, in principle, be accommodated by a narrowband transmission facility.
- to evaluate user opinions of the teleconference service and to compare these with what would be predicted from the laboratory results.

These objectives were met successfully by using a microwave link and audio lines to connect the specially prepared conference rooms in Hartford and in Willimantic, a distance of 40 km (approximately 45-60 minutes travel time). The teleconference facilities included simultaneous two-way television, two-way audio communication and a two-way facsimile link allowing hard copies of text and graphics to be exchanged. Ten different business and government organizations participated in nine conferences ranging from half an hour to two hours in duration over a two-day period. All of these conferences involved the conduct of business having real significance to the participants and which, in a few cases, would not have been possible without the teleconference setup. The overall response to the tests was favourable. There does seem to be a need for teleconference services, possibly operated on a shared basis, even between locations separated by no more than about 45 minutes' travel.

"The Field Trial of Audio Conferencing with the Union Trust Company."
NRS Reference 305, July 1974

Between December, 1973 and May, 1974 NRS conducted a field trial of an experimental teleconference system. The system was tested between the Stamford and New Haven Executive Offices of the Union Trust Company, a large Connecticut bank chain. The purpose of the field trial was two-fold:
1. to determine the acceptability and effectiveness of teleconferencing as an alternative to travel for face-to-face meetings by management
2. to measure the effects of teleconferencing on communication between the two executive offices.

Specially-designed speakers permitted the listener to hear the stereophonic effect, regardless of his position in the room. A facsimile device provided graphics transmission. Inter-connection of the two terminals was, initially, by Class A audio-grade telephone lines; near the end of the field trial, these were replaced with less expensive Class C voice-grade lines which were evaluated as equally acceptable.

A total of twenty-four senior management personnel at Union Trust were regular participants in the field trial, which began on December 3, 1973. They were members of various management committees who, until that time, had alternately been travelling to Stamford or New Haven for their regular committee meetings.

The evaluation of the field trial provided information on four basic dimensions of users' responses to teleconferencing:
1. users' *attitudes* or *feelings* toward teleconferencing *before* using the system
2. users' *attitudes* or *feelings* toward teleconferencing *after* first use of the system, and at other points during the field trial
3. users' *beliefs* or *cognitions* about teleconferencing, compared with face-to-face meetings
4. frequency of use of the teleconference system, as a substitute for face-to-face meetings.

The data gathering phase of the field trial lasted until the end of May, 1974, for a total of six months during which approximately 70 teleconferences were held.

In summary, the results were:

1. Before using the system, participants expected teleconferencing to be an acceptable medium for conducting meetings.
2. After using the system, users evaluated teleconferencing as acceptable, with little change in acceptability over time.
3. Teleconferencing was perceived by users as being *as effective* as face-to-face communication for most meetings.
4. Use of the system was high. Between 50 and 80 percent of what had previously been face-to-face meetings was conducted using the teleconference system. The greatly-reduced travel saved the bank between $500 and $750 per month depending on usage. (Travel costs included mileage costs, as well as the cost of executive travel time.)

Further, the monthly cost associated with teleconferencing (that is, depreciation of equipment and monthly charges for telephone lines) was offset by a ratio of more than four to one by the savings associated with not having to travel for face-to-face meetings.

FOOTNOTES

1. *Communications Technology for Urban Improvement.* National Academy of Engineering, June 1971
2. "Office Communications Analysis of the Motor Vehicle Department of the State of Connecticut," and "Office Communications Analysis of the Corrections Department of the State of Connecticut", in *New Rural Society Project,* Fairfield University, Connecticut, 1975
3. Tomey, J. F.: "The Field Trial of Audio Conferencing with the Union Trust Company", in *New Rural Society Report,* Fairfield University, Connecticut, July, 1974 (see abstracts)
4. Spirak, J.: "Federal Project Eases Rural Doctor Shortage By Dispatching New Medical-School Graduates". *The Wall Street Journal,* 19 November 1974
5. Kaufman, H. F.: "Toward an Interactional Conception of Community" in Rolan L. Warren (ed): *Perspectives on the American Community* Rand McNally, Chicago, 1973, p. 63
6. Nisbet, R.: "Moral Values and Community". *Perspectives on the American Community,* op. cit. p. 87
7. Hilewick, et. al.: *Socio-economic Impact of Investment in Transportation and Communication.* U. S. Dept. of Transportation, 1976, pp. 115-123

NRS REPORTS

"A Matrix Method for Classifying Communications Devices and Systems" *NRS reference 204,* June 1972

"The Communications Factor in Dispersal: An Overview by JUPR," *NRS reference 205,* October, 1972

BIBLIOGRAPHY

National Growth Strategy

1. Berry, B. J. L.: "The Emerging Urban Region in America." *The South African Geographical Journal,* Vol. 55 No. 1., July, 1973, pp. 3-13
2. ——: "The Geography of the Unites States in the Year 2000." *Transactions of the Institute of British Geographers,* Vol. 51, 1970
3. ——: *The Human Consequences of Urbanisation.* Macmillan, London, 1973
4. ——: *Growth Centres in the American Urban System.* Ballinger, Cambridge, Mass., 1973
5. Browett, J. G., R. F. Haswell and R. A. Rosing: "Spatial Models, Techniques and Strategies of Regional Economic Development. A Selected Annotated Bibliography." *Occasional Paper No. 5,* Dept. of Geography and Environmental Studies, University of the Witwatersrand, Johannesburg, 1971
6. Fair, T. J. D.: "Decentralization, Dispersal and Dispersion." *The South African Geographical Journal,* No. 1. Vol. 56, April 1974, pp. 94-96
7. Friedman, J.: *Urbanization, Planning and National Development.* Sage Publications, Beverley Hills, 1973
8. Friedman, J.: *Regional Development Policy.* M. I. T. Press, Cambride Mass, 1966
9. Perloff, H. S. and L. Wingo: *Natural Resource Endowment and Regional Economic Growth.* Reprint No. 24, Resources for the Future, Washington D.C., 1960

Quality of Life

1. Harvey, D.: *Social Justice and the City.* Arnold, London, 1973
2. Mishan, E. J.: *Costs of Economic Growth.* Penguin, Harmondsworth, 1967
3. Runciman, E. G.: *Relative Deprivation and Social Justice.* Routledge and Kegan Paul, London, 1961
4. Smith, D. M.: "An Introduction to Welfare Geography." *Occasional Paper No 11* Dept. of Geography and Environmental Studies, University of the Witwatersrand, Johannesburg, 1973
5. Smith D. M.: *The Geography of Social Well-being.* McGraw-Hill, New York, 1973
6. Tomaselli, K. G.: "Social Justice: Some problems at the Interface." *Probe,* 1973-4, pp. 35-38

CONCLUSION

Ardrey: Buckminster Fuller—a critique

Keyan G. Tomaselli

Frequently man is presented with the promise of new media and new ways of using currently available hardware. The future is often portrayed as a technological wonderland in which communication techniques have cheaply and painlessly solved major social, economic and educational problems. An examination of history, current information and the logic of the situation, however, reveals less optimistic expectations.[1]

Science Fiction

While many of the ideas presented in this volume may appear to delve into the realm of science fiction, one futurist considers this genre of such great importance that he has described it as ". . . the relevant literature of our time . . ."[2] Originally science fiction took the form of narrative which supported an *eigenweltliche* logic and order, was pragmatic and idealistic, was sustained by a mystique in technology and a belief in the desirability of a mathematical order in human affairs.[3] New science fiction is concerned with fantasy, alternative worlds and fictions.

By the end of the twentieth century the spatial and social dimensions delimiting the post-industrial society will have matured. It is difficult if not impossible to predict accurately the kind of living, working and entertainment environments which may supersede the post-industrial state. Science fiction writers, architects, futurologists, film-makers and artists have applied their diverse talents to this task and have proferred numerous alternative visions ranging from the controlled system-maintaining society described by George Orwell in *1984* to man's ability to arrest and control some elements of the natural order, as portrayed in the film *Zardoz*. In this film most of the action occurs in a technological commune whose members have discovered the secret of eternal life. This innovation, however, only succeeds in providing the means whereby this future "vortex community" unwittingly imprisons itself in a self-perpetuating deathless physical and social state from which a natural desire and longing for death arose. The consequent release from the sterile constraints of immortality brings with it a sense of relief and inner peace.

According to the director, John Boorman, the moral of this film is aimed at futurologists, "Too often, it seems to me, they ignore the power of evolution itself to upset the equation. Some new mutation, something we encounter on the way, some unimagined factor can change the course ahead. Science and logic are not infallibles. Paradox has a poetry of its own. For example, my vortex people have forgotten what death is like and, as a result, life has lost its vital savour. It is a psalm to paradox, a knee bent to the cruel majesty of nature.''[4] The film *Rollerball* similarly displays a ray of hope when the controlling mechanism is defeated. In the Rollerball society of the year 2018, rigid social control is effected through an equilibrium maintaining system. By the year 2000, hunger, pollution, overpopulation, militant nationalism, crime and political corruption will have been eliminated, while material comfort for all will be achieved through a well-ordered managed society dominated by the major conglomerate corporations which control the food, energy, luxury, transport and communications. Rollerball, an institutional sport of brutal physical contact functions to provide the masses with a vicarious outlet for violence and hostility. This sensory mechanism is of sufficient variety to cope with and sublimate any disturbances which may impinge upon the social system and works to maintain a state of de-differentiation and sameness in the Rollerball society. The theme of hope is activated when Jonathan E who has become a national folk hero, defies the management or controlling mechanism's order to retire before he becomes too famous. His stubborn independence is a threat to their carefully controlled comfort-orientated society. He survives and turns to advantage an ultimate institutional attempt to have him killed during a ruleless rollerball game. Consequently he introduced a disturbance which the control mechanism cannot handle and which leads to the re-introduction of some diversity (the identification of a sports hero) in an otherwise undifferentiated society.

In contrast, the ''New Images of Man'' exhibition held in the New York Museum of Modern Art[5] in 1959, portrayed a singular devastating vision as to the future of human society. Of a total of fifty artworks exhibited, only one inspired a feeling of hope. Images of man presented him amputated, decapitated, without ears, with lacerated feet, as alienated and bewildered, and facing an impending psychological and physical deterioration. Guilt and death were portrayed alongside intimations of thermonuclear disaster. Similarly, recurrent themes of much science fiction literature are apocalyptic visions of impending social disaster, of absolute devastation in which survivors are tested in terms of uncontrollable external forces.

If the future is seen in terms of disaster, what of the present? The dawn of man, the paleocybernetic age, the new media, the technotronic society, the post-industrial state, the global village and technoanarchy are all concepts which describe an increased state of human awareness and expanded consciousness, made possible through the process of communication.

Contempary developments in new communications technologies fit onto the historic trend that was originally traced by such elements as the printing press, the pony express, the telegraph and the telephone. The new media have been made possible through almost invisible electronic components, which are increasingly influencing life at all levels of existence. Data processing systems, telex communication, telegraphy and other signalling networks are the arteries of business and administration and have permeated the fabric of modern civilization. By 1970, more than half the United States work force was employed in information occupations.[6] In 1975, a national ratio of 68 telephone stations per 100 inhabitants was the norm.[7] By 1980, only 22% of the labour force is expected to be employed in manufacturing industries.[8] With the new electronic environments made possible by the prospects of holography and other laser technologies, a quality of presence may be introduced to telecommunications meetings which will be comparable to the intimacy of the boardroom, even though the participants may be spread between Frankfurt, Paris and New York. Rationalized planning, integrating transportation networks and telecommunication facilities will relax many of the locational constraints which previously determined the siting of business and industry. Already aspatial trends are operating and settlement patterns in the United States are spreading over the continental surface, localized at those places where the climate and landscape are pleasant. Population densities are settling down at the scale of the ex-urban fringes of the Eastern metropolitan areas, while household communications apparatus will be more sophisticated than that which is currently in use at the White House.[9]

Entertainment and fun places will provide facilities and possibilities even beyond the limits and innovations set by Walt Disney in Disneyland and Disneyworld. The World Expo's, the Fun Palace,[10] the Astro Mechanicool[11] and smaller temporary exhibitions such as the Cybernetic Serendipity Exhibition[12] and Hyperspaces[13] are only the forerunners of electronic experiential environments where three-dimensional holographic images and multichannel sound will interact with random human movements, where sound and light define the physical and perceptual environment.

Innovation diffusion: some impedences

The diffusion of an idea through a society does not guarantee its acceptance. A given population is not always easily convinced of the greater merits of using new communications technologies at the expense of the systems which are currently in use. It is also unlikely that electronic environments will automatically supersede face-to-face interaction. The traditional mechanisms which facilitate and encourage social interaction such as the pub, the coffee shop, societies, clubs and meetings will continue to be influential long after even the most sophisticated communications technologies have been accepted. Nilles *et al.*,[14] for example, demonstrated that, despite the relative advantage of attending lectures via telecommunications instead of driving to the campus, respondents still preferred to attend class in person and thereby to optimize social contacts. Further, the compatibility of innovations with existing values, experiences, attitudes and needs is positively related to the adoption process. The current status of AT & T's innovation of the picturephone is a case in point. This device has not achieved the expected acceptance in the United States, partly because of cost, but mainly because visual telephone contact is thought to conflict with society's concept of the nature and function of the telephone.[15] Again, despite the high potential of cable television, the predicted communications revolution whereby every person would be plugged into the world has not yet occurred. High initial investment costs, institutional barriers, the lack of an adequate subscriber base, conflicting federal and local government regulations and pressure from the broadcast industry have impeded the spread and development of TV's electronic umbilical cord.[16] This lack of investment has led one writer to comment, ". . . the building of a nationwide, satellite, microwave, cable-connected system probably won't materialize in the foreseeable future".[17] Another study investigated the feasibility, cost effectiveness and acceptability of telecommuting in Los Angeles with the information intensive industry of insurance. Telecommuting was defined as the dispersing of work functions from a central location to remote work centres closer to the workers. The results indicated that telecommuting was feasible, cost-effective and had a significant impact on energy used during commuting. Acceptability of the system was, however, somewhat limited, with factors such as educational level influencing acceptance of the communication alternative. The preference for travel was more due to subtle psychological factors of the destination than to the specific shortcoming of the communication technology.[18] This technology/human consciousness dichotomy has been placed in perspective in Price's statement, ". . . we know precious little about the value of television over radio, or colour over black and white, of television or radio over print, and of increased human relationships over all of them".[19]

Media scientists and futurists

Despite the sometimes hostile attitudes of society to new communication techniques, many of the systems discussed in the foregoing pages already exist and are subject to increasing proliferation and utilization. Many of the new media were only dreams or tracts of science fiction when McLuhan first astounded the world with *Understanding Media* and *The Gutenberg Galaxy*. More than a decade of research later, media scientists are not much closer to understanding McLuhan's prophecies of the electronic age. Indeed, Tudor[20] has even gone so far as to accuse media researchers of seeking sanctuary in a self-confirming simplified framework of macro-sociology where elements that do not fit the mass culture thesis were conveniently ignored.

The futurist establishment is now a firmly entrenched and clearly recognizable body and representative examples are included in journals such as "Futures" and an increasing number of readers such as Alvin Toffler's book, *The Futurists*.[21] The immature stage of this discipline is amply illustrated by the lack of opposing opinions, weak critical dialogue and recourse to conjecture and speculation, while basic questions remain unanswered. Toffler's bestseller, *Future Shock*[22] is an imaginitive and provocative tome which contains an almost overpowering array of information and statistics, bordering at times on what may justifiably be described as science fiction. Although this book is a compelling sociology of the future, it does fall short of a thorough investigation in certain areas. His reading of some of the available references (in terms of the total literature available on that subject) tends to lead his conclusions and leaves his arguments open to charges of superficiality and lack of depth. Bell has charged Toffler's term "future shock" as being deceptive. His basic criticism concerns the differences in the rate of change experienced between 1850 and 1940, the present and the future. Bell asserts that more change was experienced during the 70 years since 1850 when railroads, steamships, telegraph, electricity, telephone, automobile, motion pictures, radio and aeroplanes were introduced, than in the period which assumes importance in Toffler's theory.[23] Other than television, there has not been one major innovation which has affected the daily life of the individual as much as the above-mentioned innovations. Bell, however, appears to have missed the point, television *is* the most important of these inventions. Ubiquitous, influential, capable of screening electronic impulses ranging from two-dimensional monochrome pictures to three dimensional holographic colour images, it has the capacity, as previously intimated, to alter the spatial, social and economic structure of cities, business, administration and leisure time activities. The innovation itself will not cause change, but rather its implementation and the new physical and social environments which it will create to replace the old. The New Rural Society project is based on this assumption; that is, that all inventions have already been made and that the task now is one of implementation.

Ultimately, Bell's information-based post-industrial society will depend, to a significant degree, on communications services described in this book. Increasing access to an ever proliferating number of public access cable channels may well lead to a variety of future shock. The idea behind public access television is that anyone should have the opportunity to produce, direct, or hold forth on his own television programme.[24] Subjects vary from amateur soapbox opera imitations to special interest audiences such as the Gay Activist Alliance[25] and even pornographic "art" video shows.

The development and refinement of existing and new communication technologies will have to be linked with research in other disciplines such as architecture, townplanning, regional science, sociology, and psychology. Although social patterns are likely to be radically altered as a result of innovations in lifestyle and living environments, architects in particular seem to pay scant attention to the social and psychological effects of their proposals on society. They have produced a number of hypothetical future city designs which are no longer beyond the bounds of present technology. Many of these designs are synthesized in Peter Cook's[26] somewhat disjointed and all-too-brief account of twentieth century experimental architecture. The futuristic planning approach appears to be confined to only a few experimenters who believe that the future city must have technological structures radically different from those of present cities. The first settlement of this new world is already in the process of being built on 1 600 hectares in the Arizona desert. This city, named Arcosanti, is based on the arcology (a combination of architecture and ecology) notions of Paulo Soleri and represents ". . . the unmistakable expression of man the maker as man the creator."[27]

In physical terms arcology rejects the horizontal nature of the flat city and aims rather at an urban solid of superdense human vitality. A conventional city of 1 000 km^2 would be rendered instead by a hexahedron 1 km^3 in volume where distances are measured in terms of walking times. The compactness of the structure conserves land with about 90% of the area devoted to open space. Other projects still in the planning stage are the Plug-in City of the Archigram Group, the Bridge Structure of Friedman, the Marine Cities of Kikutake and Kobayshi, the Domed Cities of Buckminster Fuller, the Helical City and the Walking City.

It is perhaps significant that Cook's exposition is obviously written for architects who already possess some considerable knowledge of the works he covers and who understand that strain of jargon peculiar to architects. Not surprisingly then, his most vociferous critics are drawn from the ranks of architects. Only once does Cook mention the sociological aspects of living in such cities, and even then he only alludes to a particular sociological implication (of dubious relevance) that people don't seem to worry about the mediocrity of the dwellings they live in.[28] Rechristening the Plug-in City, one architect, no doubt with his plug in his cheek has taken Cook's Archigram Group to task and has indulgently overstated his case in the process:

"Is Archigram's Plug-in City in fact Drug-in City, the sub-conscious herald of capsule society, the ultra and last nihilist statement of world architecture, a vast web of plastic wombs in which man's limbs rot away and his brain, drug injected, blows up to fill the capsule home until, finally, the brain no longer in control of the machinery it has so carefully set up over the milleniums of years, gets sucked down the waste tube."[29]

Cook reports on architectural visionaries who appear, to a surprisingly high degree, to be developing their respective projects independently of and in contradiction to the aspatial forces which are presently determining the spatial organization of the society of the future. Their designs in the main appear to be predicated upon a lack of space, hostile environments and a vertical integration of working and living spaces. Such constructions may certainly be of value in overpopulated areas, deserts, ice environments and even the moon, but at this point will only serve a novel or experimental function in the post-industrial society.

The *Utopia or Oblivion*[30] disciples led by Buckminster Fuller and his adherents who thrive on the repetition of his jargonistic terminology have been more successful in preparing man for his confrontation with and control of the future. Their "comprehensivist" approach is eclectic and cannot therefore be considered a rigorous analysis. The contribution of this school, as with that of McLuhan, lies basically in their efforts to create in man a psychological climate to accommodate the kind of influences that individuals may experience in the future. Fuller believes that the new media and new technologies can function to separate man from the present and invalidate his past. In so doing, man will have at his disposal the mechanisms to redistribute society's scarce resources on an equitable and deserving basis. His numerous articles, books and inventions all fall back on the same basic theme: that efforts to perpetuate disparities between the rich and the poor are the result of an ancestral mentality, and that technology can work to open the gates of abundance and happiness.

Although Fuller, like Darwin, places his emphasis on the mind and not the brain, their respective arguments diverge dramatically on the mind/instinct relationship. Fuller totally rejects Darwinian theory on biological determinism and attempts to throw Malthus and his scarcity apostles out with the bathwater. Darwin's research led him to believe that mind and civilization are of little use, if, in the end, man's animal endowment will determine his ultimate fate. Robert Ardrey has modified Darwin's original assertions, positing that human intelligence and symbolic communication assist man in his capacity to relate past to future, to foresee contingencies, to evaluate, and to imagine solutions. These abilities draw on a power flowing from an evolutionary main event, even though the human mind does incorporate unlimited investigative powers as moderator in the eternal instinctual debate. The human mind, Ardrey argues, stands free and uncommitted, and is not consequent upon a single given instinct. The paradox lies in the mind's dependence on the outcome of the interaction of all the human instincts. The most pervasive, significant instinct of man is his urge to develop ever better and more devastating weapons. In terms of this hypothesis, the process of civilization may be regarded as a dynamic compensatory sublimation of man's killing imperative, and rests on the most ancient of animal laws – that of commanding order.

The ascendence of civilization corresponds closely to man's increasing ability to kill – the one cannot exist without the other.[31] Ardrey's comparison of man to animal society is absolute, however hard man tries to delude himself. ''Civilization'', says Ardrey, ''lacks nothing in its imitation of nature; what it lacks, and lacks only, is its recognition of man as an animal.''[32] The Fuller/Ardrey antithesis then, revolves around the question of human nature. Each side has marshalled an impressive army of generals to win its point. Ardrey can include Lorenz, Tinbergen and Morris; while Fuller can draw on the more encompassing resources of McLuhan, Youngblood, the futurists and science fiction writers. The latter group hold that human nature is adaptable, is shaped and conditioned by fictions, media and other influences and that human survival is independent of a genetically inherited killing imperative and therefore that life in highly sophisticated city forms is ultimately realizable. Ardrey's opinions are based on the presumption of the unchanging animal nature of man.

Hence the importance of the study of ethology or animal behaviour which may be extrapolated to illuminate man's present and future behaviour. This concept has no place for the futuristic visions of the experimental architects or those scholars who, like Fuller, have urged a redirection of our consciousness, if mankind is to progress. The all-or-nothing arguments of Fuller are similar, although more optimistic than the Ardrey school which foresees nothing short of at least partial thermonuclear destruction. The result, Ardrey predicts, will be an inhibition in the further use of such weapons and a consequent darkened threshold for society, through which man may never return. His central human dream, personified in the superior weapon will have been shattered. Deprived of the contest of weapons man must find new dreams, new dynamics, new experiences to absorb him, new means of resolving his issues and of protecting whatever he holds as good. His survival depends on this search, or he will find himself lost. Governments will lose their force and societies their integration. Ardrey, in a severe attack of pessimism, is not very hopeful:

"Must the city therefore perish in a blinding moment of universal annihilation? Was the sudden union of the predatory way and the enlarged brain so ill-starred that a guarantee of sudden and magnified disaster was written into our species' conception? Are we so far from being nature's most glorious triumph that we are in fact evolution's most tragic error, doomed to bring extinction not just to ourselves but to all life on our planet?"[33]

In other words, the genetically pre-programmed nature of man will preclude his mind or consciousness from exerting control over his predatory and territorial animal instincts. If this is so, then the answer to Ardrey's questions is Yes. An alternative option to the above conclusions is to be found in Desmond Morris's contribution, *The Human Zoo*. His submission to the Darwin-Ardrey hypothesis is total, although his emphasis and conclusions differ:

"In what promises to be the more crowded world of the future, they (the politicians, administrators, etc.) must become good biologists as well, because somewhere in all that mass of wires, cables, plastics, concrete bricks, metal and glass which they control, there is an animal, a human animal, a primitive tribal hunter, masquerading as a civilized super-tribal citizen and desperately struggling to match his ancient inherited qualities with his extraordinary new situation. If he is given a chance he may yet contrive to turn his human zoo into a magnificent human game park. If he is not, it may proliferate into a gigantic lunatic asylum."[34]

A more recent parallel concept, sociobiology, the study of the biological basis for social behaviour in every species, ran into a cloud of marxist fallout at the 1976 Meeting of the American Anthropological Society. Labelled by its detractors "as an attempt to justify genetically the sexist, racist and elitist status quo in human society", the antagonism level monitored was reminiscent of the churches' denunciation of Galileo. For this reason alone, the concept may snowball and ultimately survive as a valid method of analysis despite the book burning pogroms of its hysterical egalitarian minded persecutors.[35]

The constant and somewhat dubious comparison of man and human society with the behaviour of rats, termites, sea birds, chimpanzees, monkeys, and gorillas, and of his built environment to a zoo or territorial imperatives tends to relegate all philosophical discussion to a zero level and conveniently evades the possibilities of the evolution of a new strain of *homo sapiens* which may be able to enlist its mind in the control of instinct. Such a creature may yet become integrated in a future society where socio-minds, developed to the degree postulated by Siff, may become the norm, although, as Mallows clearly points out, the majority of people may never attain this ability. Ardrey cannot deny that such a mutation is possible, and that their enlightened control of society may well avert the impending holocaust. *Rollerball* describes one such society.

The Utopia chimera

Unfortunately Fuller, in company with many professed Utopians, does not concern himself with either an adequate definition or a measurement of the concept of happiness. A number of writers have tackled his thorny problem with inconclusive results. Smith proposes the notion, "social well-being" and defines it as ". . . the specific end of a continuum of abstraction that descends from human happiness through the concept of the quality of life to social well-being".[36] Although the pursuit of happiness is of fundamental social concern, this notion requires philosophical explanation because scholars agree neither on its substance nor its source. Galbraith cites Bertrand Russel [37] in this connection, ". . . a profound instinctive union with the stream of life," but, as Galbraith remarks, ". . . we do not know what is united".

To agree that the purpose of science is to improve society in order to achieve what Bentham has phrased, ". . . the greatest happiness of the greatest number . . ." is essentially simplifying the issue and evading the operational difficulties in its application as an optimal welfare function. Does the scientist standardize a happiness level and then try to achieve this for the greatest number, or should a maximum welfare level be identified to benefit the greatest number? Another writer, perhaps with a tongue in the cybernetic cheek, constructed the following definition: "The amount of happiness is the quotient of all that is attained at a given moment, and all that is consciously and unconsciously desired at that given moment". That is:

$$G(t) = -\log \frac{\dfrac{dA(t,W)}{dt}}{\dfrac{dW(t,A)}{dt}}$$

Where: G = amount of happiness
   A = all that is attained at a given moment
   W = all that is consciously and unconsciously desired at that moment
   G,W and A are functions of time (t)[38]

The equation represents a situation where happiness depends on how far our desires are fulfilled at a given moment. Two alternatives exist in order to compute the highest possible value for G. These two opposing approaches delineate the methods by which the Eastern and Western worlds search for happiness. The East has attempted to optimize the subject equation by minimizing the denominator, by making the wishes smaller in order to achieve their fulfilment. The West, in contrast, has tried to optimize the subject equation by making the numerator always bigger and bigger. Changes in this equilibrium can be directly attributed to, amongst other influences, the effects of the media.

Information rich versus information poor

A major problem associated with the application of new communications technologies is its tendency towards unbalanced development. Although communications capacity has increased tremendously over the last few years, this increase has benefited institutions and businesses rather than the public, and the urban, rather than the rural regions of the country.[39] The problem is stated: "In an urban technological society the difference between those with, and those without access to new communication and information-handling devices, often produces a difference between a group that controls its own affairs and a group that is totally dependent on the paternalistic benevolence of information handlers."[40] In other words, new communication techniques and technologies create new information gaps before old gaps close, i.e. the information poor group is increasingly left behind with the introduction of each new communication technique.

Considerable differences also exist between developing countries and modern economies. Although the gap, for example, between countries with a high proportion of telephones and those with comparatively few is decreasing, on a world basis the telephone population ratio remains at less than 10 telephone stations per 100 inhabitants. While the information orientation of industrial and post-industrial civilizations may increase human awareness amongst their respective populations, the same information can exert negative influences on information poor societies, who, although included in the global information network or noosphere, are nevertheless not actively part of that network. Mead [41] provides an example of this kind of separation,

". . . At the time that a New Guinea native looks at a pile of yams and pronounces them 'a lot' because he cannot count them, teams at Cape Kennedy calculate the precise second when an Apollo mission must change its course if it is to orbit around the moon". Mead has identified three basic types of culture which have relevance for an analysis of society from the traditional to the post-industrial.

1. At the lower end of the continuum are *postfigurative* cultures in which children learn primarily from their forebears. Change is slow and imperceptible, so much so, that grandparents cannot conceive of any other future for their grandchildren than their own past lives. On the passing of traditional society Daniel Lerner writes, ". . . *inertia* was the modal principle of personality for most people. It is not that traditional people did nothing, on the contrary, many of them worked as hard and as long as their oxen. It is rather that they did nothing *new*. What sustained traditional society . . . was the routinization of life-patterns in a self-sealing system that required no ingenuity and rewarded no initiative from its population. Rooted in their place and pride, traditional mankind lived by their constraints—unaware of them as constraints, because no communications alerted them to alternatives. Modernization . . . reversed all this".[42] In other words the system maintaining propensity of traditional society was disturbed by one or a combination of modernizing influences resulting in change from inertia to one of experimentation. The statement "we have always done it this way" developed in an evolutionary and sometimes revolutionary direction, to "there must be an easier and more efficient way." Traditional social systems usually exhibit a built-in resistance to change, have low literacy, poor understanding of scientific methods and remain relatively isolated because of poor communication links. Often communication in support of change has no common ground or basis of understanding with the receiving culture. Congolese soldiers, for example, during World War II, meeting Donald Duck for the first time, threw stones at the screen because they thought they were being ridiculed. "Animals don't talk," they shouted. "Whoever saw a duck in uniform?"[43]

Traditional societies in contact with other cultures will only survive if they can achieve internal stability or homeostasis. Life continues only until it begins to decay more quickly than it can reconstruct itself.

The last two centuries have shown only too often that there are limits to the rate of cultural change, and that beyond a certain point the pressure of an alien culture results in internal collapse of the native life without assimilation of the new.[44] The amount of happiness, if defined as a measure of the adaptability of a cybernetic system at a given moment will lead to the establishment of an equilibrium between desires and what can be attained at a given moment. If this delicate balance is upset, societal decay will proceed faster than adaptation or reconstruction. A classic example is Sharp's account of the indiscriminate supply by missionaries of steel axes to stone age Australians.[45]

The stone axe was a fundamental piece of cultural equipment in that it helped relate men, women and children to nature and technological behaviour; it served the purpose of transforming natural into cultural equipment, and defined person to person contact. The uncontrolled diffusion of steel axes, operating in conjunction with other elements also being introduced from the white man's several subcultures undermined the realm of traditional ideas, sentiments and values without defining new conceptions to replace them. The result was a mental and moral void which fore-shadowed the collapse and destruction of all Yir Yorant culture, if not, indeed the extinction of the biological group itself. The Yir Yorant society, once a local enclave of increasing organization maintained by the process of homeostasis, became subject to a reversible information transfer from the general stream of increasing entropy, was unable to adapt to such disturb-ances and consequently degenerated into a state of increasing chaos and dedifferentiation. The happiness equation could not correlate desires with fulfilment, the error control signal was unable to prevent the communi-cation of disturbances, and the variety in the decision making or controlling mechanism could not match up to the alien influences communicated by the missionaries.

2. Postfigurative cultures generally overlap with *cofigurative* cultures which, for our purposes, are the result of the development of new forms of technology in which the old are not expert and where the experience of the young generation is radically different from that of their parents, grand-parents, and other older members of their immediate community. The young have to develop new styles based on their own experience and thereby provide models for their own peers. Cofiguration occurs mainly in develop-ing or modernizing societies and the demands on communications are proportionately greater than at any other stage of social growth. Communi-cation is exhorted to help survey a new environment, raise people's aspir-ations, guide and control a dynamic process, teach new skills and socialize citizens to a new and different society that is still only in the process of becoming.[46] In a modern society a certain degree of change is anticipated and the behaviour of each new generation is expected to differ from that of the preceding generation; in a modernizing society, change assumes the proportions of an overriding national value, and therefore planned and

purposeful use of communication ranks highly. The relationship between communication and the modernizing process raises many problems of which two will be dealt with.

(a) Since the majority of innovations which diffuse through a modernizing society are most probably first introduced by imitation from outside the country rather than by local invention, the process of international innovation diffusion is important also for the spread of economic development within that country. In many of the less developed countries, while new techniques and ideas are accepted and adopted with relative ease in the capital cities, they do not spread to the lower levels of the urban hierarchy or to the rural areas.[47]

(b) The mass media possess the "multiplier property" which functions to produce productive development attitudes rapidly.[48] The media are able to impart new skills and new values with relative ease. According to Lerner[49] they have performed this task all too well, which is why mankind now faces a revolution of rising expectations. People have assimilated new desires and demands, their aspirations and expectations have risen, the media have taught people what to *want*. The result is that when all desires for the moment are attained, more desires immediately emerge. In this case the media have optimized the subject equation by making the numerator always greater, so as to obtain everything possible. What the media have not done is to teach people how to *get*. Lerner does offer some general though vague guidelines to bring the want:get ratio into a dynamic equilibrium. People, he says, must be taught not to expect things they cannot get, that reward will follow effort and that productivity is the source of goods. The regulatory mechanism of the mass media in conjunction with natural communications allies such as schools, religious organizations and work associations should co-operate in providing people with a reliable guide to a better reality.

3. In *prefigurative* cultures the future of society can no longer be seen as an extension of the past. The high level exchange of information from one social system to another has increased the rate of change or negentropy to a level where parents are also learning from their children. The rapid development and diffusion of communications technologies ensures that enclaves in human society are no longer isolated individual closed systems. Those societies which are unable to adapt and survive are not endowed with adequate decoding mechanisms or social institutions to cope with the new information input. Like the stone age Australians, new information cannot be assimilated, information is lost in transit, and Western man or the innovators who induce changes appear to be unable to control this loss or predict the consequences that their technologies may have on such tra-

ditional or modernizing societies. Interaction between postfigurative and prefigurative societies is perforce dominated by confusion, impotence and ultimately, confrontation. The Habitat '76 United Nations Conference on Human Settlements, for example, yielded an insight into the structure of this confusion. Editorial comment, published in *Futures* reads: "The poor may have found it politically expedient to denounce the rich in public, but in private, relations seemed much more harmonious than one might have expected. There seemed to be a common vocabulary and a recognition of common problems."[50]

Hallen's report was more pessimistic, "The confusion of ideas, the thousands of interests and causes all shouting to be heard at the Forum at Vancouver reminded me of the day after God and his action committee had dealt the builders of Babel their comeuppance. An erudite intellectually alert world set within a technology of enormous communications possibilities has solved the problem of the old historical and social languages. For today the new languages are of ideas, of concepts and of causes. Men are now separated more by the ideas they hold than by the historical language they speak."[51] In other words the same generations living at the same point in time live in essentially different but overlapping cultural epochs, all of which represent different interpretations of overlapping realities. Reality and future assume a symbiotic relationship, and definition depends more upon a given society's position on the postfigurative-prefigurative continuum, than on semantic construction. For as Bell asserts, for most of human history reality was *nature* – to find shelter from the elements and to wrest food and sustenance from the soil, the waters and the creatures. Then reality became *technics*. The Industrial Revolution was an effort to substitute a technical order for the natural order. In the industrial society the cosmological vision was the game against fabricated nature. The post-industrial society is not concerned with either nature or technics. *Reality is primarily the social world* where men live more and more outside nature, and less and less within the machinery of things; they live with and encounter one another.[52]

Similarly other definitions will change depending on a society's location on the reality matrix. Architecture, for example, originally a response to the need for adequate shelter was broadened to include other aspects such as religion, status, protection, functional specialization and aesthetics. Today architecture draws heavily on the social sciences, the physical sciences and electronics. To modify Cook's assessment: music and other sounds, lights and other things seen, media and electronic audio-visual environments, and almost any kind of physical support will be an integral part of architecture within the next decade. The central thesis of Youngblood's exposition is a redefinition of cinema to mean ". . . a process of becoming, man's ongoing historical drive to manifest his consciousness outside his mind, in front of his eyes".[53]

According to Mead, the paths by which man entered the present can never be traversed again. Coming by different roads out of the past, all the peoples of the earth are now arriving in the new world community. In this respect, Mead's thoughts converge with those of Fuller, ". . . The freeing of man's imagination from the past depends . . . on the development of a new kind of communication with those most deeply involved in the future—the young who were born in the new world . . . the development of prefigurational cultures will depend on the existence of a continuing dialogue in which the young, free to act on their own initiative, can lead their elders in the direction of the unknown." Mead concludes, ". . . we must recognize that we have no descendants as our children have no forebears . . . The Future is Now!"[54]

The post-industrial society postulated by Daniel Bell has emerged, the concept of the noosphere has become a fact, the wired city may eventually become the wired nation and the metasocio-mind may become reality, but man's consciousness has not yet caught up with his technology. The technology/human interrelationship still remains, however, unclear. Teer has posed the question of who should be consulted in the search for clarity. He states, "Having made a quick check by rereading in retrospect the transactions of former symposia on the future, I have the impression that the artist and the philosopher have a better developed 'clairvoyance' than the technologist and the sociologist".[55] This statement is strengthened if credence is paid to the phenomenon whereby an increasing number of academics are seriously studying the literary importance of science fiction. In the United States alone, over 200 schools, colleges and universities offer courses on science fiction.[56] Working within total experimental freedom, the science fiction artist is not restricted to any particular discipline or method of enquiry, his works may exhibit the same precise logic and rigorous attention to detail as a scientific endeavour, but he is not constrained by scientific determinism. If science fiction is a window to the future then the impressions conveyed in the literary historical development suggests some hope for mankind, for in surveying science fiction literature over a period of many years, at least one reviewer has monitored an optimism in future thinking that is becoming less of a rarity than it has been in the past, particularly for those people working on creative visions of alternative societies.[57] Science and art and a convergence of the two into the technological artist may ultimately explain the relationship between man and his technology and media and change.

FOOTNOTES

1. Bell, S. and G. A. Bogatz: *The First Year of Sesame Street. An Evaluation.* New Jersey Educational Testing Service, Princeton, 1970
2. Livingston, D.: "Science Fiction Survey." *Futures,* Vol. 8. No. 4, 1976, p. 361
3. Baxter, J.: *Science Fiction in the Cinema.* Paperback Library, New York, 1970, pp. 1-13
4. Quotations taken from *Production Notes,* Twentieth Century Fox
5. Selz, P.: *The New Images of Man.* The New York Museum of Modern Art in collaboration with the Baltimore Museum of Modern Art, Doubleday, New York, 1959
6. Hilewick, C. L. *et al.: Socioeconomic Impact of Investment in Transportation and Communication.* U.S. Dept. of Transportation, 1976, p. 19
7. Siemens International Telephone Statistics, 1976
8. Bell, D.: *The Coming of the Post-Industrial Society.* Heineman, London, 1974, p. 133
9. Berry, B. J. L.: "The Emerging Urban Region in America." *The South African Geographical Journal,* Vol. 55. No. 1, 1973, pp. 3-13
10. See *Architectural Review,* January, 1965
11. See P. Cook, *Experimental Architecture.* Studio-Vista, London, 1970, pp. 138-151
12. Cybernetic Serendipity Exhibition, Institute of Contemporary Arts, London, 1968
13. "Hyperspaces exhibition," *Architectural Design,* July 1969, pp. 383-4
14. Nilles, J. M. *et al.: Telecommunications – Transportation Tradeoffs.* Univ. of Southern California Press, Los Angeles, 1974
15. Dickson, E. M. and R. Blowers: "The Video Telephone. A new Era in Telecommunications: A Preliminary Technology Assessment." *Ithaca,* Cornell University, June 1973
16. Branscomb, A. W.: "The Cable Fable: Will it Come True?" *Journal of Communication,* Vol. 25 No. 1, 1975, pp. 44-56
17. Ibid., p. 55
18. Milles, J. M. *et al.;* op. cit.
19. Price, N. E.: "The Illusions of Cable Television." *Journal for Communication,* Summer, 1974, p. 74
20. Tudor, A.: *Image and Influence.* Allen & Unwin, London, 1974, p. 138
21. Toffler, A. (ed.): *The Futurists.* Random House, New York, 1972
22. Toffler, A.: *Future Shock.* Pan Books, London, 1972
23. Bell, D.: *The Coming of the Post-Industrial Society.* op. cit., p. 318
24. Doty, P.: "Public Access Cable TV: Who Cares?" *Journal of Communication,* Vol. 25 No. 3, 1975, pp. 33-41
25. Wurtzel, A.: "Public-Access Cable TV: Programming." *Journal of Communication,* Vol. 25 No. 3, pp. 15-21
26. Cook, P.: *Experimental Architecture.* Studio Vista, London, 1970
27. Soleri, P.: *Arcology: The City in the Image of Man.* The M.I.T. Press, Cambridge Massachusetts, 1969
28. See H. Gans: *The Levittowners.* Penguin, Harmondsworth, 1967
29. Hodgkinson, P.: "Drug-in City," *Architectural Design,* Vol. 29 No. 11, 1969, p. 586. Also see J. Tarn's exergetic dedication of 26 verses: "The Gospel according to Archigram." *RIBA Journal,* May 1973, p. 245
30. Fuller, R. B.: *Utopia or Oblivion.* Penguin, Harmondsworth, 1969
31. Ardrey, R.: *African Genesis.* Collins, London, 1961, pp. 345-346
32. Ardrey, R.: *The Territorial Imperative.* Collins, London, 1967, p. 344
33. Ardrey, R.: *African Genesis,* op cit., p. 318
34. Morris, D.: *The Human Zoo.* Jonathan Cape, London, 1969, p. 248

35. See *Time* report, Dec. 13, 1976, p. 72.
36. Smith, D. M.: *The Geography of Social Well-Being.* McGraw-Hill, New York, 1973, p. 66
37. Galbraith, J. K.: *The Affluent Society.* Pelican, Harmondsworth, p. 280
38. Irtem, A.: "Happiness, Amplified Cybernetically" in J. Reichardt (ed.): *Cybernetics, Art and Ideas,* Studio Vista, London, 1971, pp. 72-75
39. Hilewick, C. L., E. J. Deak, K. K. Kohl and E. Heinze: "Socioeconomic Impact of Investment in Transportation and Communication." *Final Report, U.S. Dept. of Transportation,* August 1976, p. 20
40. Katzman, N.: "The Impact of Communication Technology: Promises and Prospects." *Journal of Communication,* Vol. 24 No. 4, 1974, pp. 47-58
41. Mead, M.: *Culture and Commitment,* Panther, London, 1970
42. Lerner, D. and W. Schramm (eds.): *Communication and Change in Developing Countries.* East-West Center Press, Honolulu, 1967, p. 306
43. Doob, L.: *Communication in Africa: A Search for Boundaries.* Yale University Press, New Haven, 1961, p. 289
44. Forde, C. D.: *Habitat, Economy and Society.* University Paperbacks, London, 1966, p. 472
45. Sharp, L.: "Steel Axes for Stone Age Australians," in E. H. Spicer (ed.) *Human Problems in Technological Change.* Wiley & Sons, New York, 1967, pp. 69-90
46. Lerner and Schramm, *op. cit.*, p. 6
47. See Hilewick *et al.,* p. 29
48. Oshima, H. T.: "The Strategy of Selective Growth and the Role of Communications," in Lerner and Schramm, *op. cit.* pp. 76-91
49. Lerner and Schramm, *ibid.* pp. 305-317
50. Blair, T.: "Habitat without Settlement." *Futures,* Vol. 8 No. 4, 1976, p. 229
51. Hallen H.: "Thoughts from the Habitat Conference." *Institute of South African Architects: Newsletter,* No. 2, 1976, p. 8
52. Bell, D.: *The Coming of the Post-Industrial Society.* op. cit., p. 488
53. Youngblood, G.: *Expanded Cinema,* Studio Vista, London, 1970, p. 41
54. Mead: *op. cit.,* p. 119
55. Teer, K.: "Information in 1984." *Australia Telecommunications Research,* Vol. 7 No. 3, 1973, pp. 48-53
56. George, H.: "Science Fiction, Mankind's Early Warning System." *Futures* Vol. 5 No. 5, 1975, pp. 491-494
57. Livingston, D.: "Science Fiction Survey." *Futures,* Vol. 7 No. 5, 1975, p. 441

GLOSSARY OF TERMS

Cybernetics

cybernetics: The science of control and communication in an organism or organization, natural or technological. It incorporates the study of messages as a means of controlling society.

chaos: the 2nd Law of Thermodynamics implies that the ultimate state of any system is disorder or chaos. Chaos is a state of sameness of components and conditions in a system.

control: intervention which corrects deviations from certain goals within a system.

disorder: same as chaos.

disturbance: an influence which may cause deviation from a system's state of equilibrium.

entropy: a measure of the degree of order or disorder existing in any system based on the distribution of energy.

feedback: an output signal which is returned to the input to influence the relationship between input and output.

homeostasis: the functioning of a system so as to correct adverse disturbances through the detection of deviations from the desired state; it involves correction by negative feedback.

information: a pattern of energy used for communication or control within a system.

netagive feedback: this signal tends to diminish deviations or errors in transmitted messages and leads to stability of a system.

negentropy: a state of increasing order.

order: the opposite of chaos or disorder, a state of increased differentiation.

positive feedback: this signal tends to increase deviations and causes instability or change.

sensory mechanism: a device which is sensitive to different forms of energy (e.g. information) in a system.

system: a group of interacting, interrelated, or interdependent elements forming a collective entity.

variety: for effective regulation in any system, the variety in the decision making mechanism or control device must be at least equal to that of the disturbances.

General

bioelectric: electrical impulses occuring within a living organism.

diachronic: the study of a sign-system in an historical evolutionary, linear system.

distance decay: the fall-off of attraction (e.g. a stopping centre) with increasing distance.

exoskeleton: a skeleton external to the body, e.g. a motor car, a computer.

friction: the impedence of motion.

kinesics: a discipline based on structural and descriptive linguistic models to describe communicative behaviour of the human body.

meme: similar to noogene.

mentation: mental processes or function.

noo (Greek) pertaining to mind.

noogene: thought patterns generated by minds and transmitted nonbiologically from mind to mind and generation to generation to ensure the persistence of concepts, philosphies and behaviour patterns.

noosphere: Chardin defined this as the terrestrial sphere of thinking substance. Despite Chardin's rejection of Asian thought, this notion
appears to be based on the ancient Hindu philosophy, the *Akasha*, a
sanskrit word relating to the Universal Mind, from which all matter is
derived. (Term coined by Youngblood.)

paleocybernetic: The psychological transistion from the Industrial Age to the
Cybernetic Age, or Post-Industrial Age. The Age when man is free to
discover what and who he is and when he gains the ability to manifest
his mind in front of his eyes. Similar to Chardin's concept of convergence and the *Akasha* notion of the Universal Mind.

paradigmatic: those elements which occur among the potential (or ''absent'')
elements of a statement.

semiology: the study of sign systems as a communicative medium.

surface: a geographical term describing a stylized graphical interpretation of
specific data (e.g. marketing or consumer).

synchronic: the study of the condition of a sign-system at a given stage.

synergistic: the process whereby individual components interact and combine to produce a system whose performance is greater than the sum of
the contributions of its separate parts.

syntagmatic: those elements which exist among the actual (or ''present'')
elements of a statement.